HALFWAY HOMEMADE

HALFWAY HOMEMADE

MEALS IN A JIFFY

PARRISH RITCHIE

THE COUNTRYMAN PRESS

A division of W. W. Norton & Company

Independent Publishers Since 1923

Copyright © 2017 by Parrish Ritchie

For information about permission to reproduce selections from this book,
write to Permissions, The Countryman Press,
500 Fifth Avenue, New York, NY 10110

For information about special discounts for bulk purchases, please contact
W. W. Norton Special Sales at specialsales@wwnorton.com or 800-233-4830

Manufacturing by QuadGraphics, Taunton
Book design by Chin-Yee Lai
Production manager: Devon Zahn

Library of Congress Cataloging-in-Publication Data

Names: Ritchie, Parrish, author.
Title: Halfway homemade : meals in a jiffy / Parrish Ritchie.
Description: New York, NY : Countryman Press, a division of W. W. Norton &
Company, Independent Publishers Since 1923, [2017] | Includes index.
Identifiers: LCCN 2016058311 | ISBN 9781682680704 (hardcover)
Subjects: LCSH: Quick and easy cooking. | LCGFT: Cookbooks.
Classification: LCC TX833.5 .R56 2017 | DDC 641.5/12—dc23 LC record
available at https://lccn.loc.gov/2016058311

The Countryman Press
www.countrymanpress.com

A division of W. W. Norton & Company
500 Fifth Avenue, New York, NY 10110
www.wwnorton.com

10 9 8 7 6 5 4 3 2 1

TO

SAM & DEAN

my boys,
my babies,
my heart,
my greatest
accomplishments.

CONTENTS

❧ INTRODUCTION ❧

When I was younger I imagined myself as a mom. I would picture myself wearing heels and an apron in the kitchen, mashing potatoes before pulling a roast out of the oven and topping it with homemade gravy. The kids are in the living room coloring while my husband sits at the table, ready to carve up the roast. And then we all sit down to this fabulous dinner, ending with a slice of pie I made completely from scratch.

Then I grew up, and I had kids, and life took a different turn. At 6 o'clock I find myself scrambling to get dinner on the table. The heels and apron from my fantasy have been replaced with leggings and a messy bun. The kids are in the kitchen pulling at my legs, adamantly refusing to eat anything besides dinosaur-shaped chicken nuggets. While my reality may be a little different from my fantasy, I wouldn't have life any other way. And thanks to a little help from the grocery store shelf, I can get delicious meals on the table in no time.

I have been cooking since I was 13 years old, when I watched my first episode of *Martha Stewart Living*. I started creating recipes then. The dishes in this book are tried and true recipes, some from my family and some that I created myself. As a busy mom, I love to take long or hard recipes and figure out how I can make them easier. In a world where so many dishes call for quinoa and spiralized vegetables, I wanted to share my easy recipes with everyone. So I started my blog, *Life with the Crust Cut Off*, embracing canned biscuits, condensed soup, and whipped topping. These are real recipes for real families: recipes anyone can make and everyone will love. Just because a recipe calls for premade ingredients doesn't mean it can't create a beautiful dish, and just because a dish is beautiful doesn't mean it's hard to make. The recipes on my blog and in this book are how I am able to get delicious home-cooked food on the table every day. They are simple, gorgeous, and above all delicious.

The Starting Line

CHILI CHEESE FRY DIP

CHICKEN ALFREDO DIP

HOT ARTICHOKE DIP CUPS

KOREAN BBQ WINGS

CREAMY GARLIC CUCUMBER SANDWICHES

BAKED SOUTHWESTERN EGG ROLLS

SPICY SHRIMP SHOTS

CHICKEN ENCHILADA CUPS

EASY CHICKEN POT STICKERS

BBQ CHEESEBURGER MEATBALL BITES

BBQ BACON CHICKEN CUPS

HAWAIIAN PIZZA BITES

SLOW COOKER KOREAN MEATBALLS

CHEESY RANCH PULL-APART BREAD

RANCH TURKEY CLUB PINWHEELS

MEXICAN RESTAURANT WHITE DIP

BACON CHEESEBURGER DIP

CRAB AND CORN SALAD CUPS

RANCH CRACKER MIX

SPICY SAUSAGE BALLS

CHILI CHEESE FRY DIP

Serves 4 to 6

1 pound lean ground beef

One 1-ounce packet chili seasoning mix

One 15-ounce can red kidney beans, drained

One 15-ounce can diced tomatoes with green chilies

One 8-ounce block cream cheese, softened

1 cup shredded Cheddar cheese

Waffle fries or waffle chips, for serving

QUICK!

You can make this easy dip even faster by using canned chili! It is also a great way to use up leftover chili.

Who doesn't love chili cheese fries? They were a huge craving of mine during my first pregnancy, which resulted in many late-night excursions for a large chili cheese fry and a cherry limeade. This dip is a delicious spin on chili cheese fries that everyone will love. I serve it with waffle-cut fries or waffle-cut chips. Sometimes on the weekend my husband, Dan, and I will settle down with a few movies and this chili cheese dip. It is the perfect binge-worthy food. If you have any leftovers, they make a great topping for tostadas at lunchtime (page 125).

1. Preheat your oven to 350°F.

2. Brown the ground beef in a medium skillet, drain when cooked through, and then add in the chili seasoning, beans, and tomatoes.

3. Spread the softened cream cheese across the bottom of a pie plate. Top the cream cheese with your chili mixture and with the shredded cheese.

4. Pop the pie plate into the oven and cook for 15 to 20 minutes, until the cheese is melted.

5. Serve with crispy waffle fries or waffle-cut potato chips.

CHICKEN ALFREDO DIP

Serves 4 to 6

It is no surprise that people love chicken Alfredo—it is creamy, cheesy, and of course delicious! It is my sister's favorite, so one night, when we were having Italian at my grandparents, I wanted to bring an appetizer that fit with the theme, and—*voilà*—this dish was born. It is big on flavor and takes just minutes to throw together, thanks to the jarred sauce. I love serving it with toasted bread slices, but if you're trying to be all healthy I guess you could serve it with veggies, too. The leftovers are perfect served over pasta (if you even have leftovers!).

2 cups shredded cooked chicken

One 8-ounce block cream cheese, softened

1 jar Alfredo sauce (about 14 ounces)

2 cups shredded mozzarella cheese

Grated Parmesan cheese

Crackers, pita chips, toasted baguette slices, or veggies, for serving

1. Preheat your oven to 350°F.

2. Mix the chicken with the softened cream cheese, Alfredo sauce, and 1½ cups of the mozzarella. Place the mixture in a glass pie dish or an 8-inch square glass baking dish. Top with the remaining mozzarella and a sprinkling of Parmesan.

3. Bake for 20 minutes, until the dip is bubbly.

4. Serve with crackers, pita chips, toasted baguette slices, or veggies.

QUICK!

Use your favorite canned or rotisserie chicken to save even more time.

HOT ARTICHOKE DIP CUPS

Makes 2 dozen

One 14-ounce can artichoke hearts, water-packed, drained and chopped

1 cup mayonnaise

1 cup grated Parmesan cheese

1 garlic clove, minced

One 8-ounce can crescent roll dough or one 8-count can crescent rolls

Scallions, chopped, for garnish

Artichoke dip is a classic appetizer. It uses very few ingredients and is always a favorite. I love to take classics and update them with a little twist, a new spin! That's why I came up with these dip cups. You might be thinking artichoke dip is a little retro, but it will always be a crowd-pleaser! Plus, everything retro comes back around—'70s bell bottoms, '80s crimped hair (let's just hope the '90s fashion doesn't!). These perfectly poppable little bites of flaky dough and rich artichoke dip are a fabulous combination and perfect for any party!

1. Preheat your oven to 350°F. Grease a 24-well mini muffin tin.

2. Mix all of the ingredients except the crescent rolls until thoroughly combined.

3. Unroll the crescent roll dough or crescent rolls. If using crescent rolls, press the seams together to make four rectangles. Cut the dough into 24 squares.

4. Place one square of dough in each muffin well and spread it up the sides. Fill each crescent cup with the dip, being careful not to overfill them.

5. Bake for 20 to 25 minutes, until lightly browned.

6. Garnish with scallions.

TIP: You can throw some thawed and drained frozen spinach in the mix, too!

KOREAN BBQ WINGS

Serves 4 to 6

¾ cup soy sauce

1 tablespoon rice wine vinegar

1 cup brown sugar

¾ cup cola

2 garlic cloves, chopped

4 to 6 scallions

2 to 3 pounds frozen chicken wings, thawed in fridge

My mom and I used to love watching this particular show about a family and their eight kids. One time they made *bulgogi*—Korean BBQ beef—and we just had to replicate it! I dug up a few different recipes, mashed them together, and came up with a marinade that I now use on everything. It is especially wonderful on these chicken wings. I keep all of the ingredients on hand to make these and they are always gone in no time. The marinade is the perfect balance of sweet and savory. But don't let the secret ingredient scare you, it is essential for the flavor and it helps caramelize the wings. This recipe is super easy and delicious, but make sure to give yourself some time to let the wings marinate in that wonderful marinade for maximum flavor.

1. Mix all of the ingredients, except for the wings, together in a bowl.

2. Place the wings in a large zip-top bag and pour the marinade over the wings. Marinate for at least an hour in the fridge—overnight is best!

3. Preheat your grill to medium-high (about 350°F) or your oven to 425°F.

4. Grill the wings for 20 to 25 minutes, until cooked through, basting occasionally. Juices from the chicken should run clear when the wings are cooked through. Watch the wings carefully because the sugars like to burn.

5. To cook the wings in the oven, place them on a cookie sheet and bake for about 40 minutes, until they are cooked through.

CREAMY GARLIC CUCUMBER SANDWICHES

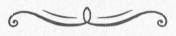

Serves 12

1 English cucumber

1 loaf fancy thin white sandwich bread

5 ounces garlic-and-herb spreadable cheese

QUICK!

These could not be any easier to make. They get a ton of flavor from the garlic and herb cheese spread (usually found with the finer cheeses at your store), and you can change up the flavor easily.

Whenever I have a girly get-together or a light lunch party I serve these sandwiches. They feel so elegant, like something every good Southern girl needs to know how to make so we have something to eat with tea and our pinkies out.

Cucumber sandwiches must be made on thin white bread with the crust cut off. I'm pretty sure that's the law around here!

1. Slice the cucumber and lay the slices on paper towels to soak up some of the excess moisture.

2. Slices the crusts from your bread. Spread a thin layer of the cheese on each slice of bread.

3. Top half of the bread slices with cucumbers and a second piece of bread. Slice the sandwiches diagonally or cut into rounds with a cookie cutter.

TIP: These should be served immediately or they will get soggy.

BAKED SOUTHWESTERN EGG ROLLS

Makes about 40

2 cups shredded cooked chicken

One 1-ounce packet taco seasoning

One 7-ounce can chipotle peppers in adobo

1 teaspoon vegetable oil or butter

1 small onion, diced

1 green pepper, diced

1 red pepper, diced

One 11-ounce can mexicorn, drained (regular corn works fine too)

One 15-ounce can black beans, drained

8 ounces shredded Pepper Jack cheese

8 ounces shredded Colby-Jack or Cheddar cheese

2 packages of egg roll wrappers (about 40 wrappers total)

Kosher salt

1 cup ranch dressing

Once upon a time, long ago, a certain fast food chain made southwestern egg rolls and they were the best things ever. I still dream of those crispy little bites of heaven. Alas, they are no more—*sigh*—so I decided to try to re-create them at home. I hate frying (not a health-conscious preference, a lazy preference), so I bake mine (you can fry yours, more power to ya) and they come out crispy and satisfy my never-ending craving for those egg rolls.

1. Preheat your oven to 400°F. Grease a cookie sheet.

2. Add the chicken, taco seasoning, and 1 teaspoon of the adobo sauce from the chipotle can to a large bowl.

3. Heat one teaspoon of oil or a small pat of butter in a medium skillet and add the diced onion and peppers. Sauté until the onions are translucent and a little caramelized, 10 to 15 minutes. Add the cooked veggies to the bowl with the chicken.

4. Mix in the drained corn and beans along with the cheeses.

continued on next page

QUICK!

Rotisserie chicken makes quick work of the filling and bottled ranch helps make a spicy sauce for dipping.

5. Place an egg roll wrapper on a clean surface with one of the corners facing you. Add a little of the chicken mixture to the middle of the wrapper, shaping the filling into a log. Begin to roll up the wrapper. Halfway through, tuck the ends in and finish rolling. Place the egg roll seam-side down on the cookie sheet. Repeat until all the filling has been used.

6. Spray the tops of the egg rolls with cooking spray and top with a sprinkling of kosher salt (very important!). Bake the egg rolls about 15 minutes, until they are browned and crispy (keep an eye on them as they can brown quickly).

7. Mix 2 teaspoons of the adobo sauce into the ranch dressing and stir to combine. Add more adobo if you really like heat! Serve with the egg rolls.

TIP: Freeze these before baking and you will always have an amazing appetizer on hand!

In my family we have lots of get-togethers. Birthday parties every other week, holidays, you name it, we are getting together for it. And if there is anything I learned being raised Southern it is that hors d'oeuvres are a must. Whether it is just a casual Sunday supper at my grandparents' or a big holiday party, people expect appetizers. Sometimes we even just have appetizers—everyone brings one and we just snack and chat all day.

When you have guests coming over, you may be tempted to set out some cheese and crackers or a bag of chips (both solid choices), but appetizers are where you can really try something new and stretch your creative wings.

SPICY SHRIMP SHOTS

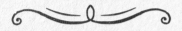

Makes 15 to 20, depending on shrimp size

½ cup mayonnaise

1½ tablespoons Sriracha

2 teaspoons granulated sugar

1 pound shrimp, steamed

Lemon wedges, for garnish (optional)

I am all about elegant-looking recipes that take no time to make, and these Spicy Shrimp Shots are it! They will be the hit of any get-together. Sometimes I am hesitant about serving shrimp for parties because people just devour them and they are gone within minutes. But with these shrimp shots, everyone gets their own little cup so there's no more wrestling at the shrimp tray. And they are as easy to make as they are to eat: Just steam or fry some shrimp and serve in a shot glass with this creamy, spicy sauce that is wonderful on anything.

1. Mix the mayo, hot sauce, and sugar together until well combined. It is better to let the sauce sit in the fridge for a few hours, but you can serve it right away if you need to.

2. Place 1 to 2 tablespoons of sauce in each shot glass.

3. Balance 1 or 2 shrimp on each glass and add a wedge of lemon, if desired. *Voilà*—super elegant in no time at all!

TIP: You can also serve these on a tray with a big bowl of sauce in the middle for dipping. Or you can serve them for dinner, like my mom. It's one of her favorites—she just makes the shrimp and sauce and eats it all over rice.

CHICKEN ENCHILADA CUPS

Makes 2 dozen

2 cups shredded cooked chicken

½ cup shredded Colby-Jack cheese

½ cup shredded Pepper Jack cheese

½ cup enchilada sauce

½ cup canned black beans, drained

One 8-ounce can crescent roll dough or one 8-count can crescent rolls

Sour cream and chopped scallions, for garnish (optional)

QUICK!

Shredded rotisserie chicken and canned enchilada sauce make these enchilada cups a super quick snack!

O kay, so everyone in my family loves enchiladas—they are a huge crowd-pleaser. My family even had an enchilada cook-off where we all made our own versions for everyone to taste and judge. We all make them differently but of course mine are best! In the end I think we all won because we got to eat a bunch of enchiladas.

Naturally I make enchiladas in every form I can, and these little cups are perfect for appetizers.

1. Preheat your oven to 350°F. Grease a 24-well mini muffin tin.

2. Mix the chicken, cheeses, sauce, and beans together.

3. Unroll the crescent roll dough or crescent rolls. If using crescent rolls, press the seams together to make four rectangles. Cut the dough into 24 squares.

4. Place a crescent square in each muffin well and press up the sides. Fill each cup with the chicken mixture, being careful not to overfill them. You can top with extra cheese before baking if you like.

5. Bake 20 to 25 minutes, until the cups are golden brown.

6. Cool slightly and serve. Garnish with sour cream and scallions if you choose.

TIP: Ground beef instead of chicken also works perfectly in this recipe!

EASY CHICKEN POT STICKERS

Makes about 20

One day I decided to go out on a limb and make something that I had always been a little skeptical to try: pot stickers. Though I knew they were delicious, they just seemed a little complicated to make. Well, guess what? They are so stinkin' easy! My mom loves these pot stickers, and thankfully with a few ingredients from the store I can whip them up anytime. The pot stickers also freeze beautifully. The filling is so good and easy and you can use it to make other things, like wontons and egg rolls.

1 pound ground chicken

3 scallions, finely chopped

1 garlic clove, minced

2 teaspoons brown sugar

½ teaspoon ground ginger

2 teaspoons rice vinegar

2 teaspoons soy sauce

Dash crushed red pepper flakes

Ground black pepper to taste

1 package wonton wrappers (about 20)

1 tablespoon butter

2 tablespoons water

Sweet-and-sour duck sauce

Sriracha

1. Flour a cookie sheet.

2. Mix the chicken, scallions, garlic, sugar, ginger, vinegar, soy sauce, pepper flakes, and black pepper in a large bowl. Transfer the filling mixture to a medium skillet and cook over medium-high heat, breaking up the chicken into crumbles as it cooks, until the chicken is no longer pink. Remove the skillet from the heat.

3. Place a wrapper on a clean surface and place 1 to 2 teaspoons of filling in the center; fold over the dough to form a triangle and seal the edges, crimping if desired. Place the pot stickers on the floured cookie sheet.

4. Heat the butter in a large skillet with a lid over medium-high heat. Add the pot stickers and the water and cover. Cook for about 3 minutes. The water should evaporate and the bottoms of the pot stickers will be brown and crispy.

5. Serve the pot stickers with the duck sauce drizzled with a little Sriracha.

TIP: Keep the wrappers covered while working to prevent them from drying out.

BBQ CHEESEBURGER MEATBALL BITES

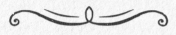

Makes 12

12 Hawaiian sweet rolls

Your favorite BBQ sauce

12 frozen meatballs, thawed

6 slices Cheddar cheese, cut in quarters

4 tablespoons (½ stick) butter, melted

½ tablespoon Montreal steak seasoning

½ tablespoon sesame seeds

½ tablespoon poppy seeds

Regardless of what the bikini-clad models on TV portray, wolfing down a big fat cheeseburger isn't the most attractive thing. However, there is nothing more satisfying. That's why I created these cheeseburger bites. You get all the big flavor of a cheeseburger packed into a dainty little roll. Plus, you can put away quite a few of these and no one will bat an eye—can't do that with full-size burgers. A little BBQ sauce, melted cheese, and soft buns make these little appetizers spectacular! A little bacon wouldn't hurt either.

1. Preheat your oven to 350°F.

2. Slice the rolls in half and place the bottom halves in a small oven-safe glass dish. Spread a little BBQ sauce on the bottom rolls and top with a quarter slice of cheese and a meatball. Top with the remaining cheese.

3. Spread BBQ sauce on the top half of the buns and place them on top of the meatballs.

4. Combine the melted butter with the steak seasoning, sesame seeds, and poppy seeds. Brush the tops of the buns with the butter mixture.

5. Cover the pan with foil and bake for 15 minutes, or until the cheese is melted and the buns are golden. Serve.

Frozen meatballs help me get these ready in minutes.

BBQ BACON CHICKEN CUPS

Makes 16

Every time my husband and I go to this particular pizza restaurant we love, I always get the BBQ chicken pizza. My husband always teases me because he knows I will never stray from my usual order. I'm in a pretty serious relationship with BBQ chicken. At home I love whipping up simple BBQ chicken breasts and serving them with a big pile of rice and black-eyed peas. Even when it's not dinnertime, I want BBQ chicken, and thus these little cups were born.

2 cups shredded cooked chicken

½ cup BBQ sauce

8 slices bacon, cooked and crumbled

1 cup shredded Cheddar cheese

8 large canned biscuits

1. Preheat your oven to 350°F. Grease 16 wells of a muffin tin.
2. Combine the chicken, BBQ sauce, bacon, and cheese in a bowl.
3. Separate the biscuits into 2 halves, place one half in each well of the muffin tin, and press the dough up the sides. Fill the biscuits with the chicken mixture, being careful not to overfill. Top with additional cheese if you like.
4. Bake for 15 to 20 minutes until golden brown.

QUICK!

These snacks are so easy to make with leftover BBQ chicken, good ol' canned biscuits, and microwave bacon! If you don't have leftover chicken, rotisserie chicken makes this dish a snap!

HAWAIIAN PIZZA BITES

Makes 16

1 cup diced ham (deli, leftover, or any ham ya got)

1 cup shredded mozzarella cheese

½ cup pineapple tidbits, drained (chop smaller if they are big)

¼ cup red onion, thinly sliced

16 large canned biscuits

¾ cup pizza sauce

When I don't order BBQ chicken pizza, I have to have Hawaiian pizza—I am that person who likes pineapple on their pizza! It is so yummy: a little pineapple, ham, and onion make the perfect pie. Now take all those ingredients and wrap them up in a flaky biscuit crust and you've got an appetizer that will wow everyone.

1. Preheat your oven to 375°F. Oil a cookie sheet.

2. Mix the diced ham, cheese, pineapple, and onion together in a bowl.

3. Roll out the biscuits to make a thinner round. Spread the pizza sauce on each biscuit, leaving a little edge. Place 1 to 2 tablespoons of filling on each biscuit. Fold the biscuit in half, pressing to seal.

4. Bake for 15 to 18 minutes until golden brown.

TIP: Serve ranch and extra pizza sauce on the side for dipping.

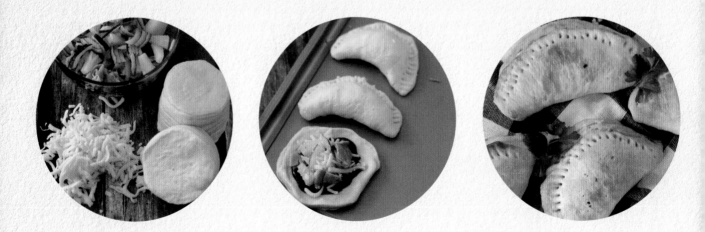

SLOW COOKER KOREAN MEATBALLS

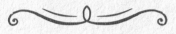

Serves 8 to 10

¾ cup soy sauce

1 tablespoon rice wine vinegar

1 cup brown sugar

¾ cup cola

2 garlic cloves, chopped

4 to 6 scallions

1 pound frozen meatballs

1½ tablespoons cornstarch

Yes, meatballs again! (Seriously, stock up on the frozen ones. They are such a great thing to have on hand.) I have found that meatballs are always a hit—at all of my holiday parties they are the first things to go—so I like to have an arsenal of meatball recipes, all made in the slow cooker, because when you're having a party the slow cooker is your best friend. This recipe is another way to use that wonderful Korean marinade that I just love. These meatballs are quick to assemble since you start with frozen meatballs, and everyone will love the Korean twist!

1. Mix the soy sauce, vinegar, brown sugar, cola, garlic, and scallions together.

2. Place the meatballs and sauce in your slow cooker. Cook on low for 4 to 6 hours or on high for 2 to 3 hours.

3. Right before serving, mix the cornstarch with about a tablespoon of water, just enough to make a slurry. Then add the slurry to the meatballs to thicken the sauce a bit.

TIP: These meatballs also make an amazing dinner served over rice.

CHEESY RANCH PULL-APART BREAD

Serves 4 to 6

1 round loaf of bread (any kind you prefer)

8 tablespoons (1 stick) butter

1 tablespoon dry ranch seasoning mix

1½ cups shredded Cheddar cheese

1½ cups shredded mozzarella cheese

8 strips bacon, cooked and crumbled

2 to 3 scallions, chopped

QUICK!

You can use microwave bacon if you're really in a time crunch.

Pull-apart breads seem to be all the rage right now. I had never made one, so I figured I would do so for a girly get-together I was hosting. Is there anything a group of women love more than bread with butter and cheese . . . and bacon? Of course, if I was going to make one, I was going to go all the way. A crusty loaf of bread is scored and filled with buttery ranch, gooey cheese, crispy bacon, and a little scallion, because a little green always makes it *feel* healthier.

1. Preheat your oven to 400°F. Line a cookie sheet with foil.

2. Cut ½-inch lines into the bread lengthwise, then widthwise, making sure you do not cut all the way through to the bottom—this is important.

3. Melt the butter and combine it with the ranch seasoning. Drizzle the melted butter between the cuts in the bread, making sure to get it in all the nooks and crannies. Stuff a good amount of cheese between the slices. Then comes the bacon—yum! Make sure to get it in all the crevices.

4. Place the loaf on the prepared cookie sheet and cover loosely with foil. Bake for 12 minutes.

5. Remove the foil from the top of the bread and bake for another 5 minutes, to get everything good and melted.

6. Sprinkle with scallions and serve warm!

TIP: This is also fabulous alongside a bowl of chili for dinner.

RANCH TURKEY CLUB PINWHEELS

Serves 12

½ pound deli turkey, chopped

8 ounces shredded Cheddar cheese

½ pound bacon, cooked and crumbled

4 to 6 scallions, chopped

Two 8-ounce cans crescent roll dough or two 8-count crescent rolls

¼ to ½ cup ranch dressing, plus more for dipping

Honey mustard, for dipping (optional)

These pinwheels are big on taste and super easy, thanks to some store-bought ingredients that will help you get these appetizers out in no time!

1. Preheat your oven to 350°F. Lightly grease a cookie sheet.

2. Mix the turkey, cheese, bacon, and scallions together in a bowl.

3. Unroll the crescent roll dough. If using crescent rolls, press the seams together to make two long rectangles.

4. Spread a thin layer of ranch on each rectangle. Place a small amount of the turkey mixture on each rectangle, covering the whole surface except for the edges—you want to leave a seam to help with sealing the roll.

5. Roll up each rectangle into a long log, sealing it at the seam. Slice the log and place the slices on the cookie sheet.

6. Bake for 12 to 17 minutes, or until the edges of the dough are golden brown.

7. Let the pinwheels cool slightly and carefully transfer them to a serving platter. Serve with ranch or honey mustard for dipping.

TIP: Make these a little spicy by subbing Pepper Jack cheese for the Cheddar.

I love Thanksgiving. We spend it at my grandparents' every year. As soon as you walk in the door, my grandma has little crystal dishes of olives and pickles set out everywhere to snack on. It's my job to bring the appetizer, and even though I would love to try making new recipes, everyone always requests these pinwheels. Don't limit yourself to Thanksgiving, though—these are perfect all year round for any occasion!

MEXICAN RESTAURANT WHITE DIP

Makes 4 cups prepared sauce

One 30-ounce jar Miracle Whip

1 cup sour cream

½ cup milk

18 pimento-stuffed olives, plus
   1 tablespoon juice from the jar

6 garlic cloves

1 teaspoon dried oregano

1 teaspoon garlic salt

1 teaspoon cumin

½ teaspoon salt

½ tablespoon red pepper flakes

½ teaspoon cayenne pepper

4 dashes hot sauce

Juice of half a lemon

Here in Virginia the Mexican restaurants have this amazing white sauce that they serve with their chips and salsa. Other Mexican restaurants don't carry this sauce, so I had a hard time finding a recipe and had to come up with my own. It makes a wonderful dip but is also amazing on tacos, nachos, a shoe—it makes everything amazing.

There is one important thing to know when making this dip: plan ahead. This dip HAS to be made 12 to 24 hours before you need it. Any less time and it will not taste like it is supposed to. It is *so* worth the wait though!

1. Easiest recipe ever! Just put all of the ingredients in your food processor and blend until they are smooth.

2. Here is the MOST IMPORTANT PART! Refrigerate this sauce for 12 to 24 hours. It needs that time to meld together or it will not taste right.

TIP: This dip goes with quite a few recipes in this book, so mark this page!

BACON CHEESEBURGER DIP

Serves 6 to 8

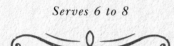

1 pound bacon, diced

1 pound lean ground beef

One 32-ounce block Velveeta cheese

1 small onion, finely diced

¼ cup milk

½ tablespoon Montreal steak seasoning

½ tablespoon Worcestershire sauce

Shredded lettuce, diced tomato, sliced red onion, and sliced dill pickles, for garnish

Ketchup and mustard, for garnish

Tortilla chips, potato chips, or bread, for serving

If there is anything I have learned it is that any dip that starts with a base of Velveeta cheese is going to be amazing. You can add anything to that loaf of melty goodness and it will create a delicious dip, so I mixed that creamy cheese with hamburger and bacon and topped it with cheeseburger toppings—perfect for dipping tortilla chips, baguette slices, or cubed bread. This dip comes together almost as fast as it disappears!

1. Brown the bacon in a large skillet. Remove the bacon from the pan and drain off the grease.

2. Brown the hamburger and diced onion in the skillet and drain off any grease. Return the bacon to the skillet.

3. Cube the Velveeta and add it to the skillet over medium heat. Add the milk, steak seasoning, and Worcestershire. Stir together on medium heat until the cheese is completely melted. Remove the mixture from the pan and place it in a serving dish.

4. Sprinkle lettuce, tomatoes, sliced onion, and pickles on top. Drizzle a small amount of ketchup and mustard over the top.

5. Serve with chips or bread.

TIP: This recipe is also awesome served over French fries.

CRAB AND CORN SALAD CUPS

Makes 2 dozen

24 mini phyllo cups (found in the frozen section)

½ cup mayonnaise

½ teaspoon Old Bay seasoning

½ teaspoon granulated sugar

One 15-ounce can corn, drained

12 ounces lump crabmeat, picked clean of shells

6 slices bacon, cooked and crumbled

Chives, sliced

My mom is obsessed with crab. We get them all summer and have huge crab feasts at my grandparents'. We all sit outside and dump bright red, steaming crabs on newspaper-covered tables, put on our bathing suits, and sit around picking crabs until the lightning bugs come out.

It is a summer tradition and a yummy one at that. But sometimes we want crab without all the mess and shells. That is why I came up with these fabulous little crab and corn salad cups. Lump crab is mixed with sweet corn and piled into little crispy cups making the perfect light appetizer!

1. Preheat your oven to 350°F.

2. Crisp up your phyllo cups on a baking sheet in the oven for 4 minutes.

3. Meanwhile, mix the mayonnaise, Old Bay, and sugar together. Add in the corn, crab, and crumbled bacon.

4. Fill the phyllo shells with the crab and corn salad. Top with chives and serve!

TIP: Grill fresh corn for fabulous flavor.

RANCH CRACKER MIX

Makes 8 cups

My grandma makes the most amazing snack mix. It often makes its appearance around the holidays. When I was younger it always seemed so special I couldn't wait for it! The holidays would finally roll around, and there, scattered around her house in little glass dishes, was this snack mix. I finally got the recipe from her and added my own twist—the little cheesy fish crackers that my kids just love. A packet of dry ranch mix is your secret ingredient to this delicious mix. I make it all the time and often have to triple the batch because my husband's friends can't get enough!

¼ cup vegetable oil

One 1-ounce packet dry ranch seasoning mix

1 teaspoon garlic salt

One 9-ounce bag oyster crackers

One 6.6-ounce bag cheese fish crackers

1. Preheat your oven to 250°F.

2. Add the oil, ranch seasoning mix, and garlic salt to a small bowl. Stir until mixed thoroughly.

3. Add the crackers to a 1-gallon zip-top bag and pour in the oil mixture. Seal the bag and toss until well coated.

4. Arrange the crackers in a single layer on an ungreased half-sheet pan. Bake the crackers for 15 to 20 minutes or until they are golden brown.

5. Cool the mix and keep it in an air-tight container for snacking!

TIP: This snack mix is also amazing with some nuts mixed in (just like my family!).

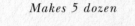
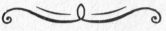

SPICY SAUSAGE BALLS

Makes 5 dozen

3 cups Bisquick or other baking mix

1 pound ground breakfast sausage

4 cups shredded Pepper Jack cheese

½ cup milk

Sausage balls are a Christmas tradition in my family. Christmas morning my mom and sister come over and make a beeline for the sausage balls for which they have been waiting all year. This year I decided to spice up the normal recipe by adding Pepper Jack cheese. With just four ingredients, these little snacks are a snap to prepare, so don't wait for the holidays to make these crowd-pleasers!

1. Preheat your oven to 350°F. Grease a foil-lined cookie sheet.

2. Mix all of the ingredients together in a large bowl. Roll the mixture into 1-inch balls and place them on the cookie sheet.

3. Bake for 20 to 25 minutes, until brown.

TIP: Let the cheese come to room temperature for easier mixing (I learned this one from my mom).

The Breakfast Club

MAPLE SAUSAGE CRESCENT ROLL-UPS

PECAN CARAMEL CINNAMON ROLL BREAD PUDDING

DENVER OMELET BURRITO

CHEESY SAUSAGE ENGLISH MUFFINS

HAM SWISS EGG MUFFINS

CREAMY MIMOSA FRUIT SALAD

BREAKFAST NACHOS

SAUSAGE GRAVY BISCUIT CUPS

MEXICAN HASH BROWN BAKE

BREAKFAST PIZZA

BACON SCRAMBLED EGG GRILLED CHEESE

STUFFED FRENCH TOAST SLIDERS

BEBE'S BREAKFAST RAMEN

HAM, EGG, AND CHEESE BREAKFAST SLIDERS

MAPLE DIJON SAUSAGE SLIDERS

CHERRY CHEESE DANISH CUPS

CHAI TEA-GLAZED BANANA NUT MUFFINS

BLUEBERRY COCONUT SMOOTHIE BOWL

S'MORES OVERNIGHT OATMEAL

BREAKFAST FRIED RICE

MAPLE SAUSAGE CRESCENT ROLL-UPS

Serves 8

16 maple sausage links

Two 8-count cans crescent rolls

3 tablespoons maple syrup,
  plus more for dipping

When it comes to breakfast food, there are people who like syrup on their sausage and people who don't. And that's cool, but the people who don't are totally missing out on some syrupy, sausagey goodness. You can add a little Cheddar or Monterey Jack cheese for a different spin.

1. Preheat your oven to 350°F. Lightly grease a baking sheet.

2. In a large skillet over medium heat, cook the sausage links until they are cooked through. Remove them from the pan.

3. Roll each sausage link in a crescent roll and place them on the baking sheet. Drizzle each roll with a little maple syrup.

4. Bake for 11 to 13 minutes or until golden.

5. Serve with extra syrup for dipping.

TIP: Some sausages come in packs of 14. If your favorite brand is packed that way, you will end up with two plain crescents left over—no harm in that!

PECAN CARAMEL CINNAMON ROLL BREAD PUDDING

Makes 12

One 8-count can large cinnamon rolls

½ cup chopped pecans

3 eggs

¼ cup milk

½ cup caramel topping

¼ cup maple syrup

Powdered sugar, for dusting (optional)

Sausage links, cooked, for serving (optional)

Once upon a time bread pudding met cinnamon rolls and they got married. As they walked down the aisle they were showered with caramel and toasty pecans, resulting in the best darn breakfast you've ever had. That's right, cinnamon roll bread pudding—life doesn't get any better!

Caramel and pecans add richness to this bread pudding. If you really want to impress, serve this in mason jars with a little sausage on top—perfect!

1. Preheat your oven to 350°F. Lightly grease 12 mini mason jars and line a cookie sheet with foil.

2. Cut each of the cinnamon rolls into 8 pieces and place them in the mason jars. Sprinkle half the pecans into the jars, reserving the other half for topping later.

3. Beat the eggs and milk together and pour the mixture ¾ of the way up the sides of each jar.

4. Place the jars on the cookie sheet and bake for 10 minutes.

5. Mix the caramel sauce and syrup together.

6. Remove the jars from the oven and top them with the caramel mixture and the rest of the pecans. Place the jars back in the oven and continue baking for another 10 minutes.

7. Remove the jars from the oven. Dust with powdered sugar if desired.

8. Skewer a few sausages, if you choose, stick them into the jars, and serve!

TIP: This recipe serves 12 as a side or 4 to 6 as a main course. You can also make this in an 8-inch square baking dish for a family-style breakfast.

DENVER OMELET BURRITO

Serves 4

2 teaspoons butter

1 cup frozen onions and peppers

1 cup cubed ham

1 cup shredded Cheddar cheese

8 eggs

Salt and black pepper

4 flour tortillas

Hot sauce or salsa, for serving

QUICK!

Frozen peppers and onions are quick and easy shortcuts here, and these burritos are great to make with leftover ham!

When I was younger my grandma would make me the most amazing omelets for breakfast, and a cheese omelet was the first thing I learned to cook in home economics. But omelets aren't the easiest things to eat, and being a busy family we often need our breakfast to go. Enter everyone's favorite way to make a meal to go—stuff it in a tortilla. Omelets go perfectly with one.

1. In a medium skillet, melt the butter on medium heat. Add the peppers and onions and sauté until they are translucent. Add the ham and warm it up. Remove the ham and veggies from the skillet and reduce the heat to low.

2. Whisk 2 eggs with salt and pepper and add them to the skillet. Cook the eggs until they are almost set.

3. When the eggs are just about set, add ¼ of the veggie and ham mixture and ¼ of the cheese. Cover the pan until the tops of the eggs are set.

4. Carefully remove the omelet from the pan and place it on a warmed tortilla (you can warm the tortillas in a microwave for 10 seconds).

5. Repeat with the remaining ingredients.

6. Roll the tortillas up and serve with hot sauce or salsa!

CHEESY SAUSAGE ENGLISH MUFFINS

Serves 6

6 English muffins, split in half

1 pound ground breakfast sausage

16 ounces Velveeta cheese, cubed

These Cheesy Sausage English Muffins are a staple in my family. My grandma started making them and then the rest of us couldn't resist. The original recipe called for Old English Cheese, which is pricey and comes in really tiny jars. Over the years we have scrapped the pricey cheese in favor of that bright orange loaf of melty cheese goodness we all love, Velveeta. This amazing breakfast only takes three ingredients and the best part is that they can be frozen!

1. Preheat your oven to 350°F (if you want to enjoy the dish right away).

2. In a medium skillet, brown the sausage and drain off any excess grease. Add the cubed Velveeta to the skillet with the sausage and melt over medium-low heat, stirring often.

3. Lay the muffins out on a baking sheet. Place the sausage and cheese mixture on each English muffin half.

4. For breakfast now, bake for 10 to 15 minutes and enjoy.

5. To save for later, freeze the muffins on the baking sheet for 2 hours or until completely frozen. Individually wrap the muffins in wax paper, place them in a freezer bag, and freeze until ready to use! When you're ready to eat them, bake them on a baking sheet for 15 to 20 minutes.

TIP: Make a bunch, wrap them up, and freeze them. They reheat beautifully and are the perfect solution for busy mornings.

HAM SWISS EGG MUFFINS

Serves 6

12 eggs

3 tablespoons milk

½ teaspoon salt

¼ teaspoon black pepper

1 cup shredded Swiss cheese

1 cup chopped deli ham

When I was pregnant with my baby Sam, breakfast *had* to be packed with protein and I became obsessed with eating eggs in the morning. Coming up with new ways to eat eggs throughout that pregnancy was rough, but these little egg cups were a lifesaver! Creamy Swiss and salty ham give the eggs all the flavor they need. They cook up in no time in a mini muffin tin, making them the perfect quick fix for breakfast any morning.

1. Preheat your oven to 350°F. Grease a 24-well mini muffin tin.

2. In large bowl, beat together the eggs, milk, salt, and pepper. Fold in the cheese and ham. Pour evenly into each mini muffin well, about ¾ of the way up the sides.

3. Bake for 10 to 13 minutes until they are set and firm. Cool slightly and serve!

4. If you have leftovers, freeze them and then just reheat for about 20 seconds in the microwave until they are warm.

TIP: Swap the Swiss for Pepper Jack if you need a little spice in your life.

CREAMY MIMOSA FRUIT SALAD

Serves 8

One 5.1-ounce box vanilla instant pudding

1 cup orange juice

1 cup champagne or sparkling wine

One 15-ounce can sliced peaches, drained

One 20-ounce can pineapple chunks, drained

One 15-ounce can mandarin oranges, drained

1 pound strawberries

4 bananas, sliced

2 cups grapes

One 10-ounce jar stemless maraschino cherries, rinsed and drained

A h, mimosas. Such an elegant excuse to drink before noon, right? My grandma always serves them in her fancy champagne glasses, and no matter how old I am I always feel more grown up drinking from them.

This fruit salad has been a staple in our family. It is easy to make and oh-so-creamy-dreamy when mixed with vanilla pudding and orange juice. This is a perfect recipe for breakfast or brunch, and since it already has orange juice it was common sense to go ahead and throw a little champagne in there, too!

1. In a large bowl, mix the pudding mix, orange juice, and champagne together. Add all of the fruit, making sure all of the fruit has been drained beforehand. Stir gently to combine.

2. Spoon the mixture into champagne glasses and chill for 2 hours.

3. Serve!

TIP: Switch it up with your favorite fruits, champagne, and fruit juice!

BREAKFAST NACHOS

Serves 4

I live for Mexican food. I can eat it morning, noon, and night. My favorite way to get that fix with my morning coffee? Nachos for breakfast! What's that you say? Oh, yes! Flavorful sausage, scrambled eggs, melty cheese, salsa, sour cream, jalapeños—anything you like—on top of crunchy tortilla chips equals breakfast perfection. I am slowly realizing that as long as you put an egg on it you can call it breakfast!

1 pound ground breakfast
   sausage

8 eggs

Salt and black pepper

8 cups tortilla chips

2 cups shredded Cheddar cheese

Choice of jalapeños, tomatoes,
   sour cream, and salsa, for
   serving

1. Preheat your broiler.

2. In a large skillet over medium heat, brown and crumble the sausage, draining off any excess grease, then set it aside.

3. Beat the eggs with the salt and pepper. In a medium non-stick skillet over medium-low heat, cook until the eggs are set.

4. Lay out the chips on a rimmed baking sheet. Evenly distribute your eggs and sausage over the chips. Sprinkle the cheese all over the chips.

5. Pop the nachos under the broiler for just a few minutes to melt the cheese, keeping a close eye on them.

6. Top with your favorite toppings and serve!

QUICK!

Brown a batch of sausage ahead of time and you can have breakfast nachos in minutes!

SAUSAGE GRAVY BISCUIT CUPS

Serves 6 to 8

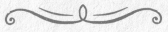

1 pound ground breakfast sausage

⅓ cup flour

½ teaspoon salt

¼ teaspoon black pepper

3 cups milk

One 8-count can flaky biscuits

Okay y'all! Being raised Southern, I know how to make spectacular sausage gravy. It has been a favorite of mine since I was little. When I used to go camping with my family, we would get up early and stop for breakfast, and I would always get the sausage gravy and biscuits. It was love! I have passed my love of this traditional breakfast down to my little sister and now I make it for her all the time. But I wanted to do something a different, so I put my delicious sausage gravy into flaky biscuit cups, because the easier it is to get that gravy into your mouth the better. The result is amazing little bites of gravy goodness!

1. Preheat your oven to 350°F. Lightly grease 16 wells of a muffin tin.

2. In a large skillet over medium heat, brown and crumble the sausage. Do not drain the grease, but add the flour to it and whisk for a minute or two, cooking the flour and creating a roux. Add the salt and pepper. Add in the milk, whisking as you do so. Continue whisking while the gravy begins to thicken and bubble. Let the gravy cook and bubble for 3 to 5 minutes while whisking until it's thick and creamy.

3. Peel each biscuit in half and place one piece in each well of the prepared muffin tin. Fill each biscuit dough cup with sausage gravy.

4. Bake for 10 to 12 minutes or until the dough is golden brown.

TIP: Make these in mini muffin tins for perfectly poppable gravy deliciousness.

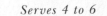

MEXICAN HASH BROWN BAKE

Serves 4 to 6

O h hash browns, how I love you! Crispy little bits of potatoey goodness are the perfect canvas for whatever ingredients you want to add. I have already told you about my love affair with Mexican food, so you won't be surprised that I wanted to add a spicy flair to my breakfast hash browns. Chorizo, peppers, onions, and a mix of cheeses make these hash browns out of this world. They are sure to wake up your taste buds!

1 pound chorizo sausage

1 cup frozen pepper and onion mix

One 30-ounce bag frozen shredded hash brown potatoes

2 eggs, beaten

½ cup shredded Colby-Jack cheese

½ cup shredded Pepper Jack cheese

½ teaspoon salt

¼ teaspoon black pepper

4 tablespoons (½ stick) butter, melted

¼ cup vegetable oil

1. Preheat your oven to 425°F. Line a baking sheet with foil.

2. In a large skillet over medium heat, brown and crumble the chorizo along with the peppers and onions. Drain off any grease.

3. Add the hash browns, sausage mixture, eggs, cheeses, salt, and pepper to a large mixing bowl. Stir to combine. Stir in the butter and oil.

4. Spread the mixture out evenly on the prepared baking sheet. Bake for 40 to 45 minutes until brown and crispy.

5. Let the hash browns cool for 10 minutes before slicing and serving.

QUICK!

Some frozen hash browns come with onions and peppers already in them, a time-saving score!

BREAKFAST PIZZA

Serves 4

6 slices bacon

2 tablespoons butter

½ small onion, diced fine

¼ teaspoon garlic salt

1 premade pizza crust

4 eggs, beaten

2 cups shredded Colby-Jack cheese

4 slices deli ham, chopped

When I was younger my mom would get us these amazing breakfast pizzas from a local grocery store. They were so good—ridiculously good, like (almost) breakfast-every-day-for-months good. Then, one day, they just stopped making them. We were devastated, so I created my own.

1. Preheat your oven to 400°F.

2. In a small skillet, cook 6 slices of bacon, then drain, cool, and crumble them.

3. In the same skillet over medium heat, melt the butter and sauté the onion until it is translucent. Add the garlic salt to the onions. Spread the onions on the pizza crust.

4. Add the beaten eggs to the skillet you used for the onions and scramble until they are just set.

5. Evenly distribute the cheese, eggs, ham, and cooked bacon all over the crust.

6. Bake for 12 to 15 minutes until the cheese is melted and the crust is golden.

TIP: The secret that really makes this pizza out of this world is the little hint of onion.

BACON SCRAMBLED EGG GRILLED CHEESE

Serves 4

8 slices bacon, cooked

Softened butter for spreading

8 slices bread

8 eggs, beaten

Salt and black pepper

½ cup shredded Cheddar cheese

8 slices American cheese

QUICK!

Use microwaved bacon to make these even faster!

One day I had the genius idea to put scrambled egg in my grilled cheese and it became an instant hit. I'm pretty sure I was making four a day when we first discovered them—my family just could not get enough. It was common sense: The only way you could ever improve on that classic grilled cheese was to add some fluffy scrambled egg to it. Then my mom had the genius idea to add bacon!

1. Butter each slice of bread on one side.

2. Beat the eggs with salt and pepper.

3. Heat a small nonstick skillet on medium-low heat, add the eggs and scramble. When the eggs are about halfway cooked, add the shredded cheese. Finish cooking the eggs. Remove the eggs and wipe out the pan.

4. Raise the heat to medium and place one slice of bread butter-side down in the same skillet. On that slice of bread place one slice of cheese, 2 pieces of bacon, ¼ of the scrambled eggs, and top with another slice of cheese. Top with another slice of bread.

5. When the first side of the sandwich is golden brown, flip the sandwich over and brown on the other side.

6. Let the sandwich cool for 3 minutes, then slice and serve.

STUFFED FRENCH TOAST SLIDERS

Serves 4 to 6

12 Hawaiian sweet rolls

One 8-ounce block cream cheese, softened

2 teaspoons lemon juice

½ cup plus 2 tablespoons granulated sugar

4 eggs, beaten

½ cup heavy cream

1 tablespoon cinnamon

Syrup and powdered sugar, for serving

I love French toast. Every time it snows (not often here in Virginia) I make it for breakfast with mugs of hot chocolate. Apparently now you can make stuffed French toast, which sounds amazing but time consuming and messy. I decided to simplify stuffed French toast with these sliders. These beauties are baked with a luscious cream cheese filling, so you don't have to stand by flipping one piece at a time.

1. Preheat your oven to 350°F.

2. Slice the rolls in half and place the bottom halves in a 2-quart baking dish or oven-safe skillet.

3. Mix the cream cheese, lemon juice, and ½ cup of the granulated sugar together until smooth.

4. Spread the cream cheese mixture on the bottom rolls. Top with the top half of the rolls.

5. Whisk the eggs and cream together. Pour the egg mixture over the sliders.

6. Bake for 25 minutes.

7. Mix the remaining 2 tablespoons of sugar with the cinnamon and sprinkle all over the sliders.

8. Bake for 10 more minutes.

9. Drizzle with syrup, sprinkle with powdered sugar, and serve.

TIP: Switch it up and add fruit!

BEBE'S BREAKFAST RAMEN

Serves 4

1 pound ground breakfast sausage

1 garlic clove, minced

2 tablespoons butter

3 scallions, chopped, plus more for serving

3 teaspoons low-sodium soy sauce

1 teaspoon brown sugar

Dash of black pepper

2 packages ramen noodles (discard the seasoning packets)

4 eggs

My sister can live off of ramen noodles; she would eat them everyday if I let her. Since she would love to eat them morning, noon, and night, I thought why not make a breakfast version. Sausage is her favorite, so this breakfast ramen is full of sausage and cheese and topped with a runny fried egg, because egg yolk rules!

1. In a medium skillet brown and crumble the sausage with the garlic. Remove the sausage from the pan and drain off any grease.

2. Add the butter, scallions, soy sauce, brown sugar, and pepper to the pan.

3. Meanwhile boil and drain the ramen noodles according to the package instructions.

4. Add the noodles to the pan. Cook for 3 minutes. Divide the noodles between bowls.

5. In another skillet, fry the eggs over easy.

6. Place one fried egg on each serving of noodles. Top with more scallions and serve!

TIP: This would be equally delicious with bacon!

HAM, EGG, AND CHEESE BREAKFAST SLIDERS

Serves 6

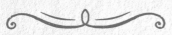

12 eggs

Salt and black pepper

12 Hawaiian sweet rolls

8 slices Cheddar cheese

8 slices deli ham

4 tablespoons (½ stick) butter, melted

1 teaspoon Dijon mustard

2 teaspoons maple syrup

QUICK!

This is a great dish to use up leftover ham!

What did we ever do before sliders? They are so quick, easy, and delicious. Ham, egg, and cheese sliders make a fantastic breakfast any time. These come together fast, and a yummy glaze brings the whole thing together!

I am addicted to ham (maybe because I'm from Virginia and we love our ham here), and I always choose ham over bacon or sausage on my breakfast sandwiches. If you are a sausage person, there is a recipe for you on the next page.

1. Preheat your oven to 350°F.

2. Beat the eggs with salt and pepper (you know how much you like in your eggs).

3. In a medium skillet, scramble the eggs until they are just set.

4. Slice the rolls in half and place the bottom halves in a 2-quart baking dish. Place 4 slices of cheese on top of the rolls in the pan followed by 8 slices of ham. Spoon your eggs evenly on top of the ham. Top with the remaining 4 slices of cheese, and then with the top halves of the rolls.

5. Mix the melted butter, syrup, and Dijon mustard together. Spoon evenly over the top of the sliders.

6. Cover and bake for 15 minutes.

7. Uncover and bake for 5 more minutes.

8. Cut the sliders apart and serve.

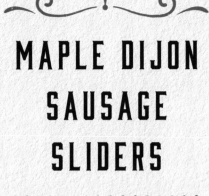

MAPLE DIJON SAUSAGE SLIDERS

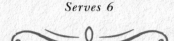

Serves 6

12 fresh sausage patties (the frozen ones are too large for this recipe)

12 Hawaiian sweet rolls

8 slices Cheddar cheese

4 tablespoons (½ stick) butter, melted

1 tablespoon maple syrup

1 teaspoon Dijon mustard

Whenever we hit the drive-thru for breakfast everyone orders sausage biscuits. I mean, how can you beat the classic fluffy biscuit and savory sausage? Oh, I know! Put that sausage on sweet Hawaiian rolls with Cheddar cheese and a simple maple Dijon glaze and you have got yourself a perfect breakfast that can be ready in minutes! My favorite part about making these sliders is that you can make 12 at a time, which means less work for this mama.

1. Preheat your oven to 350°F.

2. In a large skillet on medium heat, brown the sausage patties until they are cooked through.

3. Slice the rolls in half and place the bottom halves in a 2-quart baking dish. Place 4 slices of cheese on top of the rolls in the pan. Place one sausage patty on each roll. Top with the remaining 4 slices of cheese and the top halves of the rolls.

4. Mix the melted butter, syrup, and Dijon mustard together. Spoon this mixture evenly over the top of the sliders.

5. Cover and bake for 15 minutes.

6. Uncover and bake for 5 more minutes.

7. Cut the sliders apart and serve.

TIP: You can use maple syrup or pancake syrup, whichever you have on hand.

CHERRY CHEESE DANISH CUPS

Makes 2 dozen

One 8-ounce can crescent roll dough or one 8-count can crescent rolls

One 8-ounce block cream cheese, softened

⅔ cup granulated sugar

Splash of vanilla extract or lemon juice (optional)

2 cups canned cherry pie filling (you will need 24 cherries)

⅔ cup powdered sugar

4 teaspoons milk

Any time I make a cheesecake I nibble and nibble at it until it is gone. You can catch me at 7 a.m. with a fork in hand eating cheesecake by light of the refrigerator while I'm waiting for my coffee. Thankfully someone a long time ago created cheese Danishes, which are basically a delicious way to eat cheesecake for breakfast, but with more carbs. I figured I could make a quick version using crescent rolls, and I was right! So while I am in no way discouraging you from eating cheesecake for breakfast, I am telling you to make these soon!

1. Preheat your oven to 350°F. Spray a 24-well mini muffin tin with nonstick spray.

2. Unroll your crescent dough and press the seams together. Cut the dough into 24 squares. Place each square into a muffin well and spread up the sides.

3. Beat the softened cream cheese with the granulated sugar and vanilla or lemon, if you choose. Place some of the filling into each crescent cup.

4. Bake for 12 minutes, or until the dough is golden brown.

5. Remove from the oven and let the cups cool.

6. Into the middle of each cup place a cherry from the pie filling.

7. Stir the powdered sugar and milk together until the mixture is smooth. Drizzle the glaze over the top of the mini Danishes and serve.

CHAI TEA-GLAZED BANANA NUT MUFFINS

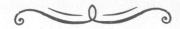

Makes 2 dozen

For the muffins

2¼ cups flour

3 teaspoons baking powder

¾ teaspoon cinnamon

½ teaspoon salt

4 very ripe bananas (the browner the better)

1 cup granulated sugar

½ cup brown sugar

6 tablespoons (¾ stick) butter, softened

2 eggs

1 teaspoon vanilla

½ cup walnuts, plus more for garnish (optional)

For the glaze

3 cups powdered sugar

1 cup chai brewed with 2 tea bags (we will not use the full cup)

Time to get a little fancy! I think the word "glazed" just means fancy, although we have glazed doughnuts and they aren't fancy. Anyhoo, I love to make banana bread. It is so incredibly moist and I can't stop slathering butter on slices and eating it all up. Sometimes I get a little crazy and make muffins, like today. I decided to make these a little fancy (glazed), so I mixed some nuts into my usual batter and made a glaze with chai tea, which is the most comforting tea flavor ever! All this together makes for an incredibly delicious, moist muffin that will make that traffic jam or carpool line a little more tolerable.

Make the muffins:

1. Preheat your oven to 375°F. Line a 24-well muffin tin with cupcake liners.

2. In a large mixing bowl stir the flour, baking powder, cinnamon, and salt together.

3. In a second large bowl, blend the bananas and both sugars together with your electric mixer. Add the eggs, butter, and vanilla to the banana mixture and blend to combine. Slowly add the dry ingredients to the banana mixture and blend to combine. Gently fold in the walnuts.

4. Fill the muffin wells halfway with batter.

5. Bake the muffins for 20 minutes, or until a toothpick inserted into one of the muffins comes out clean. Let them cool.

Make your glaze:

6. Place the powdered sugar in a bowl. Slowly add the chai tea little by little until your glaze is thick and can be drizzled.

7. Drizzle the glaze over the cooled muffins and top with walnuts if desired.

These muffins are the perfect way to use all those leftover bananas we all always have sitting on the counter. They are a delicious quick grab for mornings when we don't have time to make anything—or haven't had enough coffee to function enough to cook. Just whip up a batch of these and you've got breakfast for the week.

BLUEBERRY COCONUT SMOOTHIE BOWL

Serves 1

1 cup frozen blueberries

1 frozen banana

2 tablespoons almond butter

3 tablespoons coconut yogurt

Choice of shredded coconut, slivered almonds, lemon zest, and fresh blueberries, for serving

It sounded a little weird to me at first that people were putting smoothies in bowls, but they have become so popular I figured I should see what all the hype was about.

Wow! It's still a smoothie, but holy cow is it a pretty one! Smoothie bowls are a canvas where you can create an amazing breakfast that begs to be Instagrammed. This vibrant blueberry bowl is the perfect thing to get you energized in the morning.

1. Add the blueberries and banana to your blender and blend on low until they are chopped. Add the almond butter and yogurt and blend until the mixture is thick and creamy.

2. Pour the mixture into a bowl and top with the shredded coconut, almonds, lemon zest, and fresh blueberries.

3. Serve!

TIP: Set out an array of toppings and let everyone create their own smoothie bowls.

S'MORES OVERNIGHT OATMEAL

Serves 1

½ cup rolled oats

2 tablespoons graham cereal, finely crushed

1 tablespoon mini marshmallows

1 tablespoon mini chocolate chips

½ cup milk

Choice of graham cereal, marshmallows, and mini chocolate chips, for serving

When I was a kid I loved to eat this oatmeal that had little cinnamon gummy bears that would magically appear when the oatmeal warmed up. Overnight oatmeal is the perfect, more adult way to get some fun flavor in your oatmeal and re-create that magic. Before bed, I just put all of the ingredients in a mason jar and pop it in the fridge, and in the morning breakfast is ready: creamy oatmeal with all the flavors of that childhood classic, s'mores. Now the magic is that it all happened overnight in my fridge!

1. Add the oats, cereal, marshmallows, and chocolate chips to a ½-pint mason jar. Shake to combine, then pour in the milk.

2. Seal the jar and refrigerate over night.

3. In the morning, top with more cereal, marshmallows, and chocolate chips, and serve.

BREAKFAST FRIED RICE

Serves 4

If my mom could eat one thing for the rest of her life it would be rice. My sister shares that love. They would be perfectly content to have a big ol' bowl of buttered rice for dinner. With them in mind I came up with a way to put one of their favorite foods in a breakfast dish. I fry up leftover rice in bacon fat (oh yeah, we are going to fry some carbs in bacon grease) for the base. Then you just add in whatever you like— crumbled bacon, sausage, ham, or all three if you want. I add some frozen peas at the end for color and to make me feel better about all the bacon. Again, if you top it with an egg you can call it breakfast.

8 slices bacon, chopped

½ cup cubed ham

1 garlic clove, minced

4 tablespoons (½ stick) butter

4 cups cooked and cooled rice

2 tablespoons low-sodium soy sauce

4 scallions, chopped

½ teaspoon pepper

¼ cup frozen peas

4 eggs

Hot sauce, for serving (optional)

This is a perfect recipe to use up leftover rice.

1. In a large skillet over medium heat fry the bacon until it's crisp. Remove the bacon from the skillet and most of the grease, leaving about 1 tablespoon.

2. Add the ham to the skillet and brown lightly, then remove the ham from the skillet.

3. Add the garlic and butter to the skillet over medium-high heat. Add the rice and stir, cooking for about 3 minutes. Add the soy sauce, scallions, pepper, and peas to the rice. Add the bacon and ham. Cook for 2 more minutes, then remove the skillet from the heat.

4. Fry the eggs over easy in a second skillet.

5. Divide the rice between four bowls and add an egg to the top of each one. Top with hot sauce, if desired.

TIP: You can fry your egg or scramble an egg into the mix.

The Lunch Room

PORK BBQ GRILLED CHEESE

HOT HAM AND SWISS CROISSANTS

CHICKEN CAESAR SALAD SUBS

AVOCADO SHRIMP CLUB SLIDERS

BUFFALO CHICKEN RANCH WRAPS

CHICKEN TACO SALAD

HOGS IN A BLANKET

PULLED PORK SLAW DOGS

PIZZA NACHOS

CREAMY GARLIC-AND-HERB STUFFED POTATOES

PIMENTO CHEESE-STUFFED POTATOES

CHILI CHEESE TOSTADA

CHICKEN AND WAFFLES SALAD

POTATO CHIP-CRUSTED CHICKEN SKEWERS

CHICKEN BACON RANCH CLUB SLIDERS

BAKED CAJUN TILAPIA SANDWICHES

MEAT LOAF GRILLED CHEESE

ITALIAN SUB SKEWERS

HAM AND CHEDDAR POCKETS

ONE-POT ALFREDO MAC AND CHEESE

PORK BBQ GRILLED CHEESE

Serves 4

8 slices bread

Softened butter for spreading

2 cups shredded BBQ pork

2 tablespoons BBQ sauce

8 slices Cheddar cheese

The easiest lunches come from using leftovers that are already in the fridge. And when I have leftover pulled pork, I know the next day I am going to be having one epic grilled cheese!

Now, when it comes to grilled cheese, some people like to get all fancy and have special artisan bread—but not me. If I am having a grilled cheese, I want white sandwich bread just like when I was little. The pork and the BBQ sauce melt into that gooey cheese creating a lunch that will blow your mind and make you feel like you are wrapped up in a quilt of comfort all at the same time!

1. Spread one side of each slice of bread with the softened butter.

2. Mix the pork with the BBQ sauce.

3. On the unbuttered side of 4 slices of the bread, place a slice of cheese and ¼ to ½ cup of pork. Top with another slice of cheese and a slice of bread (butter-side out).

4. Place the sandwiches in a skillet over medium heat. Brown one side before carefully flipping to brown the other side.

5. Slice each sandwich in half and serve!

TIP: Swap out the butter for mayo for a super crispy grilled cheese—trust me!

HOT HAM AND SWISS CROISSANTS

Serves 4

2 tablespoons Dijon mustard

1 tablespoon honey

1 tablespoon brown sugar

4 croissants, split

8 slices Swiss cheese

½ to 1 pound deli ham (depending on how thick you like your sandwiches; use any flavor you like)

QUICK!

Store-bought croissants make this recipe as easy as a regular sandwich, but so much yummier!

I am a sucker for anything ham and Swiss. To me it is the best combo in the world, but that could also be because I am a ham junkie. I often keep a teeny-tiny sliced ham in the fridge to get me through the week and to stop me from having ham withdrawal. And sometimes I want to show it a good time, instead of our usual middle-of-the-night fridge dates. So I take that ham and introduce it to my friends, Swiss and croissant, and magic is made.

1. Preheat your oven to 350°F.

2. Mix the mustard, honey, and brown sugar together. Spread the honey-mustard mixture on each of the eight croissant halves.

3. Place a slice of Swiss cheese on each croissant half. Top the bottom half of each croissant with however much ham you like. Place the two halves back together.

4. Wrap the sandwiches in foil and bake for 10 to 15 minutes.

TIP: Make plenty—these sandwiches freeze well and you can heat them up to their ooey-gooey yumminess in no time!

 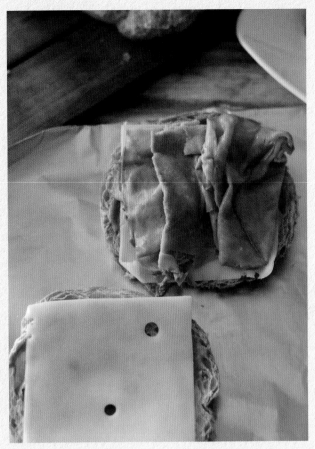

Now that I'm a mom, lunchtime is busy! Thankfully, I have whipped up some amazing recipes far beyond boring sandwiches that are super easy to make with a few store-bought ingredients.

CHICKEN CAESAR SALAD SUBS

Serves 4

4 boneless, skinless chicken breasts

Garlic salt

Black pepper

1 tablespoon butter or vegetable oil

4 submarine sandwich buns, split

Butter, softened

4 tablespoons grated Parmesan cheese

8 tablespoons Caesar dressing

2 cups roughly chopped Romaine lettuce

QUICK!

Make this sandwich even faster with rotisserie chicken.

Leave it to me to take something healthy like a salad and put it on carbs. I always thought of salads as more a "girl meal"—the boys in my life would not be happy with just a salad, so I had to make this classic salad more manly. I toast up the buns with butter and garlic salt and Parmesan cheese (I use the kind in the green canister, keeping it classy here) and pop them under the broiler to get toasty like a crouton. Then I load them up with the salad. It has easily become a favorite lunch of all the men in my life—my husband, my brother, and my boys just eat them up!

1. Preheat your broiler.

2. Sprinkle the chicken breasts with garlic salt and pepper to taste.

3. Melt your butter or heat the oil in a large skillet and cook the chicken for 5 to 6 minutes per side, until cooked through.

4. Let the chicken rest, then slice it.

5. Spread the inside of the sub rolls with softened butter, sprinkle with a little garlic salt and then sprinkle some Parmesan in there, too. Place the rolls under your broiler and watch them like a hawk until they are golden brown on the inside.

6. Spread about 1 tablespoon of Caesar dressing on the inside of each sub and lay in a few leaves of the romaine. Arrange the chicken on top of the lettuce. Sprinkle the whole sub with more Parmesan and an extra drizzle of dressing if you like.

AVOCADO SHRIMP CLUB SLIDERS

Serves 6

12 Hawaiian sweet rolls

12 frozen breaded jumbo butterfly shrimp

4 teaspoons lemon pepper seasoning

½ cup mayonnaise

12 slices microwave bacon

1 avocado, sliced thin

If I could make everything into sliders I would—I mean, they are so cute and yummy and when something is that little you can eat more and not feel guilty, right? Creamy avocado with crispy shrimp and bacon make these little clubs irresistible!

1. Preheat your oven to 425°F.

2. Remove the tails from the shrimp and discard them. Arrange the shrimp in a single layer on a baking sheet. Bake for 11 to 12 minutes.

3. Microwave the bacon according to the package directions.

4. Mix together the lemon pepper seasoning and the mayonnaise.

5. Spread 1 tablespoon of the mixture on the top half of each roll. Place one shrimp on the bottom half of each roll. Top with a slice of avocado, a slice of bacon, and the top of the roll.

6. Serve and enjoy!

QUICK!

Breaded shrimp from the freezer section is what makes this a quick lunch!

BUFFALO CHICKEN RANCH WRAPS

Serves 4

Every busy mom, parent, person—whomever—has had dinner saved a million times by rotisserie chicken. It is the true hero of the supermarket. It's cheap, it's delicious, and it can be used a million different ways. Even better, there are always leftovers to turn into lunch the next day. One day, when I was particularly pressed for time but wanted something a little different from my usual lunchtime hero, I grabbed a tortilla and spread a little ranch on it, and then added the chicken and sprinkled in some hot sauce. Then I added some cheese, because everything is better with cheese. No one is trying to make you eat your veggies, but feel free to add some lettuce in there.

2 cups shredded rotisserie chicken

3 tablespoons hot sauce

4 tablespoons ranch dressing

4 tortillas

2 cups roughly chopped lettuce

1 cup shredded Colby-Jack or Cheddar cheese

1. Mix the shredded chicken with the hot sauce in a bowl.

2. Spread 1 tablespoon of ranch dressing on each tortilla. Lay down some lettuce and divide the chicken between the tortillas. Top each one with the shredded cheese. You can drizzle on some extra ranch or extra hot sauce if desired.

3. Roll up and serve!

TIP: Play around with different cheeses. Blue cheese crumbles would be fab!

CHICKEN TACO SALAD

Serves 4

One 1-ounce packet taco seasoning

3 boneless, skinless chicken breasts (or about 2 cups leftover chicken)

4 cups chopped lettuce

1 cup cherry tomatoes, halved

One 15-ounce can red kidney beans, drained and rinsed

1 cup shredded Cheddar cheese

4 scallions, chopped

2 cups crushed nacho cheese tortilla chips

1 cup Catalina dressing, plus more to taste

When we have tacos for dinner, it is law in our family to have taco salad on the side—an addicting combo of lettuce, scallions, kidney beans, Catalina dressing, and crushed up Doritos. That's right, chips in a salad—I love my family. The best part about taco night is that the next day I get to mix that leftover salad with the leftover taco meat and make my most favorite lunch ever. Here is my version with grilled taco chicken. It's amazing!

1. Sprinkle the taco seasoning evenly over the chicken.

2. Cook the chicken in a skillet for 5 to 6 minutes per side, until it's cooked through. (You can also do this on the grill.)

3. Let the chicken rest, then slice it.

4. Add the lettuce, tomatoes, beans, cheese, chicken, and scallions to a large bowl.

5. Next comes the dressing. Add 1 cup of dressing to the mixture and toss, then add more to your liking.

6. Top with the chips right before serving.

TIP: I use Nacho Cheese Doritos, but try it with Cool Ranch or Spicy, get crazy! You can also use leftover beef instead of the chicken.

HOGS IN A BLANKET

Serves 4

One 8-count can crescent rolls

8 smoked sausages (any flavor you like; we like the cheesy ones)

8 slices Cheddar cheese

4 tablespoons (½ stick) butter, melted

Sesame seeds

BBQ sauce, honey mustard, or ranch dressing, for serving

My son Dean could eat pigs in a blanket every day, every night, all the time. He can even make them himself now. But sometimes (okay, most times) this mama is just too wiped out to stand there rolling a million little piggies in their doughy blankets.

So mama got smart.

Mama bought the big hogs.

Mama gets lunch done quick!

Mama has so much time now to do things.

Mama takes a nap instead.

What I'm trying to say is, save yourself some time and make hogs in a blanket: same delicious taste, half the time.

1. Preheat your oven to 350°F and line a baking sheet with foil.

2. Unroll the crescent dough and separate the dough into triangles.

3. Place a slice of cheese and a sausage on each crescent dough triangle. Roll up the hogs and place them on the baking sheet. Brush each one with the melted butter and sprinkle sesame seeds on top.

4. Bake for 12 to 15 minutes, until they are golden brown.

5. Serve with your choice of sauce for dipping.

TIP: There are so many flavor options with the bigger sausages, so go crazy.

PULLED PORK SLAW DOGS

Serves 4

1 tablespoon butter

½ tablespoon hot sauce

8 hot dogs

8 hot dog buns

2 cups shredded BBQ pork

2 cups coleslaw

Yes, this is another pulled pork recipe. I'm Southern, and here in Virginia it's a main food group. I don't know about other places, but around here we have slaw dogs. They are just what they sound like—hot dogs topped with coleslaw (I feel like that was pretty self-explanatory). Now, slaw dogs are delicious on their own, but what else does coleslaw go with? Pork BBQ! So it just felt natural to put pulled pork on hot dogs that have been split and browned in butter and hot sauce, and then top the whole shebang with slaw to make the most delicious, porky, Southern ménage à trois ever. So go ahead and have yourself a naughty little lunch.

1. Melt the butter with the hot sauce in a large skillet.

2. Meanwhile, split the hot dogs down the middle, being careful not to cut all the way through.

3. Place the hot dogs split-side down in the pan. Cook for 3 minutes, getting the inside nice and crispy.

4. Flip the hot dogs and cook on the other side for about 2 minutes.

5. Place a hot dog in each bun.

6. Heat the pork in the skillet until just warmed through.

7. Divide the pork between the hot dog buns. Do the same with the coleslaw.

8. Serve!

TIP: Make sure to drain the slaw well so your buns don't get soggy.

PIZZA NACHOS

Serves 4

Bag of tortilla chips

½ cup pizza sauce

2 cups shredded mozzarella cheese

Pizza toppings such as pepperoni, peppers, olives, and mushrooms

When I came up with this lunch I felt like I was creating a monster, taking parts of one junk food and mixing it with another to create some kind of Frankenstein. I quickly discovered that nachos and pizza make one delicious monster lunch! Start with tortilla chips smothered in melty mozzarella, with drizzles of pizza sauce, and then get crazy with the toppings: pepperoni, peppers, olives, pineapple, whatever you like (maybe not anchovies).

1. Preheat your broiler.

2. Lay out your tortilla chips on a baking sheet. Drizzle the pizza sauce all over the chips. Sprinkle on the cheese and top with your favorite pizza toppings.

3. Place the nachos under the broiler until the cheese just melts.

TIP: I love using the pizza sauce that comes in a squeeze bottle for this recipe.

CREAMY GARLIC-AND-HERB STUFFED POTATOES

Serves 4

4 large baking potatoes

Vegetable oil (optional)

2 tablespoons butter

Salt and black pepper

1 container garlic-and-herb
cheese spread (about 5 ounces)

Grated parmesan cheese

At every get-together my family has there is always this delicious garlic and herb cheese spread that is meant to be slathered on bread and eaten in copious amounts—which is what always happens when we're together. The spread is so delicious I of course wanted to introduce it to as many of my favorite foods as I could, including my often-boring friend, the baked potato. Man, the results were amazing! The spread has enough flavor that you don't need to add anything else, so this (almost) two-ingredient lunch comes together in no time.

1. There are two ways to cook your potatoes: oven or microwave. If you opt for the oven, preheat it to 350°F.

2. Wash the potatoes and poke them all over with a fork. If you are cooking the potatoes in the oven, rub them with oil, place them on a foil-lined baking sheet, and bake them for about 1 hour. To make this recipe even easier, skip the oven and pop the potatoes in the microwave for 12 to 15 minutes (maybe more, depending on your microwave).

3. Once your potatoes are cooked, preheat your broiler.

4. Split the potatoes in half and scoop out most of the flesh into a bowl. To the bowl add the butter and salt and pepper to taste. Add the container of cheese spread and stir all that deliciousness up.

5. Scoop the potato mixture back into the potato halves. Sprinkle a good amount of Parmesan cheese on each potato and pop them under the broiler for just a few seconds to brown them.

TIP: You can experiment with other cheese spreads—they even make spicy ones!

PIMENTO CHEESE-STUFFED POTATOES

Serves 4

4 large baking potatoes

Vegetable oil (optional)

Salt and black pepper

1 cup prepared pimento cheese

1 cup shredded Cheddar cheese

Pimentos and chopped scallions,
for garnish (optional)

QUICK!

While making your own
pimento cheese is easy,
I used premade to make
lunch a snap.

Another food group here in the South is pimento cheese. I swear, we use it like a condiment down here. Wait . . . is it a condiment, or is it cheese? Both? Neither? Who knows? What I do know is that it's delicious and makes its way into deviled eggs, potato salad, grilled cheese, and even burgers. Here I am going to show another quick baked potato recipe. I love baked potatoes for lunch because they are so easy, but they need some help in the flavor department, and that's where pimento cheese steps up.

1. There are two ways to cook your potatoes: oven or microwave. If you opt for the oven, preheat it to 350°F.

2. Wash the potatoes and poke them all over with a fork. If you are cooking the potatoes in the oven, rub them with oil, place them on a foil-lined baking sheet, and bake them for about 1 hour. To make this recipe even easier, skip the oven and pop the potatoes in the microwave for 12 to 15 minutes (maybe more, depending on your microwave).

3. Once the potatoes are cooked, preheat your broiler.

4. Split the potatoes in half and scoop out most of the flesh into a bowl. Add salt and pepper to taste. Add the pimento cheese and stir to combine.

5. Scoop the potato mixture back into the potato halves. Sprinkle each potato with shredded Cheddar cheese and pop them under the broiler for just a few seconds to brown them.

6. Garnish with pimentos and scallions, if desired.

CHILI CHEESE TOSTADA

Serves 4

4 tostada shells

3 cups leftover Chili Cheese Fry Dip (page 13)

OR 2 cups leftover chili (or 1 can chili, with or without beans) and one 8-ounce block cream cheese, softened

2 cups shredded Cheddar cheese

Remember my Chili Cheese Fry Dip from page 13? The following day I like to turn it into the most amazing lunch by putting it on tostadas with even more melty cheese. Essentially it's chili cheese nachos, but in a more lunch-like form.

1. Preheat your oven to 350°F and line a baking sheet with foil.

2. Place 4 tostada shells on the baking sheet and bake for 5 minutes, until they are crispy.

3. After baking the tostadas shells, change your oven setting to broil.

4. Place the chili cheese dip or chili and cream cheese in a microwave-safe bowl. Microwave in 30-second intervals until warm and combined.

5. Spread the chili mixture on each tostada. Top with the shredded cheese.

6. Place the pan under the broiler for just a minute to melt the cheese.

TIP: Jalapeños, green chilies, or Pepper Jack cheese can give this a kick if that's what you're into.

CHICKEN AND WAFFLES SALAD

Serves 4

4 to 6 frozen breaded chicken strips

4 frozen waffles, cut into bite-size squares

4 tablespoons (½ stick) butter, melted

⅓ cup oil

2 tablespoons Dijon mustard

3 tablespoons maple syrup

1 tablespoon vinegar

Salt and black pepper

Spring mix lettuce

QUICK!

Frozen waffles and popcorn chicken make this salad quick and delicious!

Chicken and waffles is delicious and a bit sinful, right? Fried chicken, fluffy waffles, and syrup!? It doesn't scream "healthy lunch." I like to take that decadent classic and hide it's calories with some lettuce. That's right, chicken and waffles salad! That sounds like a big oxymoron, doesn't it?

This spectacular salad is topped with a maple mustard dressing that you are going to want to drink with a straw (please don't drink the dressing with a straw unless you want to end up on one of those shows about people with weird addictions).

1. Preheat your oven to 350°F.

2. Cook the chicken strips until they're crispy, following the directions on the package.

3. Cut the chicken into bite-size pieces.

4. Mix the waffle pieces with the melted butter and place them on a cookie sheet. Bake for 7 to 10 minutes, until they're crunchy and lightly browned.

5. Add the oil, mustard, syrup, vinegar, and salt and pepper to taste to a mason jar. Shake vigorously until the dressing is thoroughly mixed. (Make sure that lid is tight!)

6. Divide the lettuce between four plates. Arrange the chicken and waffles on the lettuce. Drizzle the dressing over the salad and serve!

POTATO CHIP-CRUSTED CHICKEN SKEWERS

Serves 4

4 cups BBQ potato chips

1 pound chicken tenderloins

1 cup BBQ sauce, plus more for serving

When I was a kid, my mom used to make us the most amazing chicken nuggets. She would coat chicken in BBQ sauce and then roll it in crushed-up BBQ potato chips. I mean, when you are a kid and your mom gives you chicken nuggets that are made with potato chips, it rocks! I wanted to recreate my mom's chicken nuggets for Dean, but he is a messy boy who wants to eat messy food and lick his fingers and then touch them all over my tablet—no thank you. So I made this family favorite with chicken strips and stuck them onto popsicle sticks to keep little hands a little cleaner. Make these and serve them to your little ones or anyone who is down with potato chip-crusted chicken!

1. Preheat your oven to 425°F. Line a sheet pan with foil and spray it with a little oil.

2. Finely crush up the potato chips and place them in a shallow bowl. Place the BBQ sauce in another bowl.

3. Stick a popsicle stick in the bottom of a tenderloin and gently work it up the tenderloin. Repeat with the remaining tenderloins.

4. Dip each tenderloin in the BBQ sauce and then in the crushed chips. Place the skewers on the sheet pan. (Discard the remaining BBQ sauce and chips.)

5. Bake for 15 to 20 minutes.

6. Serve with extra sauce for dipping.

TIP: Use your favorite potato chips instead of the BBQ flavor!

CHICKEN BACON RANCH CLUB SLIDERS

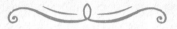

Serves 6

12 Hawaiian sweet rolls

6 frozen breaded chicken strips

¼ cup ranch dressing

6 slices bacon, cooked in the microwave

8 slices white American cheese

Since I started blogging, I have realized that if you put two particular ingredients together, people will go nuts. Two simple, everyday ingredients that, when paired together, make people drool: bacon and ranch. That's it! It's a magical combo, even better than peanut butter and jelly, bread and butter, pancakes and syrup, Slim Jims and string cheese. Wait, is that last combo just *my* family's favorite?

You can put bacon and ranch on anything and people will eat it up. I swear, try it. Got picky kids? Try bacon and ranch Brussels sprouts. Actually, that sounds like a good idea . . . keep an eye out for that recipe from me.

Anyway, these sliders are quick and delicious, packed full of flavor, and always a hit with everyone, mainly because of the bacon and ranch!

1. Preheat your oven to 425°F.

2. Arrange the chicken strips on a baking sheet and bake for 15 to 20 minutes.

3. Remove the chicken strips from the oven and cut each one in half.

4. Slice the rolls and place the bottom halves in an 8-inch square baking dish. Spread some ranch on each roll. Place 4 slices of cheese on the rolls. Place half of a chicken strip and half of a piece of bacon on each roll. Top with the remaining cheese and the top buns.

5. Cover with foil and bake for 5 minutes, to melt the cheese.

6. Serve and enjoy!

TIP: Sub any deli meat or leftover meat you have on hand for the chicken.

BAKED CAJUN TILAPIA SANDWICHES

Serves 4

½ cup cornmeal

1½ tablespoons Cajun seasoning

4 tilapia filets

4 sub buns

1 cup coleslaw

1 teaspoon Old Bay seasoning

In my family we only eat fish one way, and that is dredged in cornmeal and fried. Then we serve it with coleslaw and stewed potatoes. When I met my Louisiana-raised husband I was introduced to Cajun seasoning and now I add it to the cornmeal to make a flavorful coating. For this sandwich, I decided to bake the fish—it sounds a whole lot healthier, right? And guess what? The fish comes out of the oven unbelievably crispy. Top it with some coleslaw and this will be the only way you will want to eat your fish!

1. Preheat your oven to 425°F. Spray a baking sheet with cooking oil.

2. Mix the cornmeal and Cajun seasoning.

3. Fill a shallow bowl with water. Dip the fish in the water and then into the seasoning and place it on the baking sheet.

4. Spray the tops of the fish with spray oil.

5. Bake the fish for 15 minutes or until it's crispy.

6. Mix the coleslaw and Old Bay.

7. Place the fish filets in the subs, top with ¼ cup coleslaw, and serve.

TIP: You can certainly fry the fish if you like; we use this same recipe for our fish fry.

MEAT LOAF GRILLED CHEESE

Serves 4

If you do not take your leftover meat loaf and make grilled cheese out of it the next day, we can't be friends. It is seriously the most delicious way to eat leftovers. American cheese melts into the meat loaf, resulting in little meat-loafy bites of cheesy heaven. I honestly make extra meat loaf just to ensure we have enough for these sandwiches. These are the best things ever. Make these. Do it. Well, make meat loaf first and then do it.

Now, this is *my* recipe for meat loaf. Meat loaf recipes are like fingerprints—everyone has their own unique one, so feel free to use your own recipe for the meat loaf portion of this.

For the meat loaf

1 pound ground beef

½ small onion, grated

1 cup bread crumbs

1 teaspoon mustard

1 tablespoon BBQ sauce

1 teaspoon Montreal steak seasoning

1 tablespoon Worcestershire sauce

½ cup BBQ sauce

1 green pepper, sliced

For the sandwiches

4 thick slices cold leftover meat loaf

8 slices bread

Softened butter for spreading

8 slices American cheese

Make the meat loaf:

1. Preheat your oven to 400°F.

2. Mix all the meat loaf ingredients except for the ½ cup BBQ sauce and the green pepper.

3. Shape the mixture into one large loaf or 4 smaller loaves and place on the sheet pan. Top with ½ cup BBQ sauce and green pepper slices.

4. Bake for 40 minutes for mini loaves or 1 hour for a large loaf.

Now on to the sandwiches:

5. Spread one side of each slice of bread with butter.

6. Place a slice of cheese on the unbuttered sides. Top with a slice of meat loaf and another slice of bread (butter-side out).

7. Heat a large skillet over medium heat. Place the sandwiches in the skillet and brown one side.

8. Carefully flip the sandwiches over and brown the other side.

9. Slice diagonally and serve.

TIP: Though ketchup is the traditional topping, try BBQ sauce. It takes your meat loaf and these sandwiches to the next level.

ITALIAN SUB SKEWERS

Serves 4

My family has been going to the same sub place since I was born—it literally opened that year. This sub shop is so amazing you can honestly smell it miles away, and when you catch that whiff you know you are ordering from there for dinner.

While I will never be able to replicate their signature taste, I can come kind of close. These Italian sub skewers are a fun lunch when you want something a little "outside the box"—or bun.

This recipe serves 4 for lunch but also makes a great snack, side, or appetizer for 8.

8 slices large pepperoni

8 slices salami

8 slices ham

16 small balls or cubes mozzarella cheese

8 cherry tomatoes

16 banana pepper rings

1 sub roll, cut into 16 cubes

½ cup Italian dressing

Oregano

1. Place 1 folded slice each of salami, ham, and pepperoni, 2 pieces of mozzarella, 1 tomato, 2 bread cubes, and 2 pepper rings on a skewer. Repeat for all 8 skewers.

2. Lay the skewers in a baking dish and drizzle with the Italian dressing, sprinkle with a touch of oregano, and serve!

TIP: These can be made ahead of time; the longer they sit, the better! If you do make these skewers ahead of time, be sure to store them in the refrigerator.

HAM AND CHEDDAR POCKETS

Serves 4

When I was in high school, I loved Hot Pockets. I mean, I still do, but I don't know how socially acceptable they are for a grown woman who creates recipes for a living. So I decided to do my job and come up with a recipe that would appease my craving. The ham and cheese pockets were my jam, so of course those are the ones I wanted to re-create. Leftover ham and a ton of Cheddar (because you can never have too much cheese) are nestled into flakey crescent roll pockets and baked to melty, ooey-gooey perfection.

1 tablespoon brown sugar

2 tablespoons Dijon mustard

One 8-count can crescent rolls

8 slices deli ham

1 cup shredded Cheddar cheese

1. Preheat your oven to 350°F.

2. Mix the brown sugar and mustard together until they are combined.

3. Unroll the crescent rolls. Press the seams of two crescent rolls together to make a rectangle. Repeat with the remaining crescents.

4. Spread a thin layer of the mustard sauce on each rectangle. Lay the 2 slices of ham and ¼ of the cheese on each one. Fold the rectangle in half and pinch the edges to seal. Place it on the baking sheet.

5. Bake for 13 to 15 minutes until golden brown.

6. Serve hot!

TIP: Make a bunch using different cheeses: ham and Swiss, ham and Pepper Jack, get creative!

ONE-POT ALFREDO MAC AND CHEESE

Serves 4

My little sister is your typical teenage girl, and by that I mean she's addicted to mac and cheese. It runs through her veins and she will take it any way—fancy kinds with truffle oil, white cheddar, shells and cheese, and, in desperation, she will even scrounge out the microwave cup kinds. Interventions have failed. When she comes over for lunch there is no surprise what she wants, and I'm not going to say no because I too was a teenage girl and that lust for mac and cheese still lingers (lingers? No, it is full force). Her other vice is Alfredo, so of course it only makes sense to put two and two together in the most decadent lunch. Here's the kicker, though: It all cooks up in one pan and in no time at that!

2 tablespoons butter

2 garlic cloves, minced

3 cups water

½ teaspoon salt

1 cup evaporated milk

8 ounces shell or penne pasta

½ cup grated Parmesan cheese

3 cups Italian-blend shredded cheese

Black pepper

1. In a medium pot, melt one tablespoon of butter and add the garlic, sautéing for about 2 minutes.

2. Add the water and salt and bring it to a boil over high heat.

3. Stir in the pasta and bring back to a boil.

4. Stir the pasta occasionally for about 5 minutes.

5. Add the milk and boil for another 5 minutes.

6. Stir in the remaining tablespoon of butter, Parmesan cheese, and shredded cheese.

7. Mix well and add pepper to taste. Yum!

TIP: Add a little chicken and turn this into a fabulous dinner!

The Dinner Bell

ASIAN MEAT LOAF

CHICKEN ALFREDO RAVIOLI BAKE

MINI CHICKEN POT PIES

PHILLY STEAK ROLL-UPS

RANCH CHICKEN CLUB ROLL-UPS

ENCHILADA STUFFED SHELLS

CHICKEN PARM CUPS

COPYCAT MEXICAN MELTS

COPYCAT MEXICAN PIZZAS

LASAGNA PIZZA

SPEEDY FIRECRACKER CHICKEN

MEATBALL SUB BUBBLE UP BAKE

CHICKEN FAJITA QUESADILLAS

SLOW COOKER BEEF TIPS

PORK EGG ROLL BOWL

ONE-POT CHICKEN BACON RANCH PASTA

SLOW COOKER CARAMELIZED PORK TACOS

SOUTHERN FRIED CABBAGE WITH BACON AND NOODLES

RODEO CHICKEN WITH CREAMY JALAPEÑO RICE

QUESO CHICKEN BURRITOS

ASIAN MEAT LOAF

Serves 4 to 6

1 pound ground beef

½ cup plain bread crumbs

2 tablespoons soy sauce

½ small onion, grated

½ green pepper, finely chopped

3 garlic cloves, minced

3 scallions, chopped

1 egg

½ cup sweet and sour duck sauce

Cooked rice, for serving

My mom makes the best *lumpia*, but it is kind of a pain in the butt to make, and—oh yeah—it involves frying. So while she makes it every once in a while for special occasions, we still crave that lumpia flavor all the time. I figured there had to be an easier way to satisfy that craving. The answer? Asian meat loaf. Now, meat loaf usually gets a bad rap, right? I don't know why though, because meat loaf is friggin' delicious, especially when it has an Asian flair. I flavor mine similarly to my mom's lumpia mix (can't give away all the family secrets) and form them into mini loaves. And while old-school meat loaf usually gets a ketchup glaze, these babies get a coating of sweet and sour duck sauce! I serve it with rice instead of potatoes and it's amazing!

1. Preheat your oven to 350°F. Line a baking dish with foil.

2. Mix all of the ingredients except the duck sauce in a large bowl until they are well combined.

3. Shape the mixture into four mini loaves or one big loaf, then place your loaf or loaves on the foil-lined baking dish. Coat the top of loaf (or loaves) with the sweet and sour duck sauce.

4. Bake for 50 to 60 minutes.

5. Serve over rice.

TIP: If you want a less intense green pepper flavor, slice the pepper and lay the strips on top of the meat loaves before baking.

CHICKEN ALFREDO RAVIOLI BAKE

Serves 4 to 6

1 pound boneless, skinless chicken, diced

Garlic salt

Black pepper

1 pound frozen cheese ravioli

2 jars Alfredo sauce (about 14 ounces each)

1 cup shredded mozzarella cheese

QUICK!

If you brown the chicken in a 12-inch cast-iron skillet, you can bake the whole dish in the same skillet and save yourself some cleanup.

Some cooks plan recipes, research them, test them over and over again until they achieve perfection. Then there are cooks like me who think, "This looks good, this looks good, ohhh this is yummy," and put it all together in a pan, top it with cheese, and bake. That is how most of my recipes are born.

Chicken is good. Alfredo sauce is good. Cheese ravioli is good. All together they make an amazing, creamy, cheesy, delicious meal. It takes mere minutes to assemble and a few more minutes in the oven, so it's a busy family's dream dinner.

1. Preheat your oven to 350°F.

2. Brown the diced chicken in a skillet and sprinkle it with pepper and garlic salt. Sauté the chicken until it is cooked all the way through, then set it aside.

3. Bring a pot of salted water to a boil. Cook the ravioli according to the package instructions and drain.

4. Mix the ravioli, chicken, Alfredo sauce, and mozzarella together.

5. Place the mixture in a 9-by-13-inch baking dish.

6. Bake for about 15 minutes, until the top is slightly browned.

7. Serve with salad or garlic bread.

TIP: If your family doesn't revolt at the sight of green in a dish, add peas or spinach for a pop of color and flavor.

MINI CHICKEN POT PIES

Serves 4 to 6

½ cup canned or frozen mixed vegetables

2 cups cooked chicken

1 can cream of chicken soup

1 can cream of celery soup

Salt and black pepper

Two 8-count cans large biscuits

QUICK!

To make this recipe even easier, use rotisserie chicken. Leftover Thanksgiving turkey is also perfect in this recipe.

I love, love, love chicken pot pie. Some people make it with flaky piecrust, and other people buy the 79-cent frozen kind—my grandma makes it in a big old casserole dish topped with Bisquick. Sometimes on a chilly fall day there is nothing more therapeutic than getting in the kitchen, slicing vegetables, and making a legit, from-scratch pot pie. However, my love for pot pie is strong and requests it for dinner quite often. That is why I came up with this quick mini version. Classic pot pie filling is wrapped up in flaky, golden biscuits (canned of course!) for a quick, hearty dinner that will have you in and out of the kitchen in no time!

1. Preheat your oven to 375°F. Grease 16 wells of a muffin tin.

2. Mix the chicken, vegetables, and both soups with a little salt and pepper, to taste.

3. Carefully peel each biscuit in half. Place each half in one muffin well. Press the biscuit dough up against the sides of the well. Repeat until each muffin well contains half of a biscuit.

4. Fill each biscuit-lined well with the chicken/veggie mixture, making sure not to overfill them. Place the remaining biscuit halves on top of each well. Press the edges together to seal the mini pot pies.

5. Bake for 20 to 25 minutes, or until the biscuits are golden. Let them cool slightly before removing them from the pan.

When I am sick, move out of the way chicken noodle soup, it is a job for pot pie—which is basically like chicken soup but wrapped up in flaky dough goodness. It is the food equivalent of a hug, or of a beloved, worn quilt. It just wraps you in warmth and instantly soothes you. To me, there is no bad chicken pot pie. It is the perfect comfort food.

PHILLY STEAK ROLL-UPS

Serves 4

There is one thing you need to know about me if you want to be friends: I have a deep-rooted love for crescent rolls. See, we can be friends, but know that my BFF will always be crescent rolls. Crescent rolls always have my back. They are there when I need them, and not once have they let me down. And they make these Philly Steak Roll-Ups fabulous! This is one of my favorite quick-fix dinners because I can keep all the ingredients on hand and the flavor is always amazing. All that cheesesteak taste, but wrapped up in a flaky, buttery crescent roll—yes, girl, yes!

1 small onion, thinly sliced

1 small green pepper, thinly sliced

1 tablespoon butter or oil

One 8-count can crescent rolls

8 slices provolone cheese

8 slices deli roast beef

1. Preheat your oven to 350°F. Lightly oil a cookie sheet.

2. Heat a small skillet and quickly sauté the onions and peppers in butter or oil until they are tender and lightly caramelized.

3. Open the rolls and separate them into 8 triangles.

4. Fold a slice of provolone in half and lay it on the wide end of each triangle. Top both with a few peppers and onions, then add a slice of roast beef. Roll up everything and place it on the prepared cookie sheet. Repeat this process for all 8 crescent rolls.

5. Bake for 10 to 12 minutes, or until they are light golden brown.

TIP: You can cook up some thin-sliced steak for this recipe, too. I love how quickly you can make this dinner with roast beef!

RANCH CHICKEN CLUB ROLL-UPS

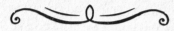

Serves 4

2 teaspoons butter or vegetable oil

Salt and black pepper

8 chicken tenderloins or strips from a breast

16 slices bacon

Two 8-ounce cans crescent roll dough or two 8-count cans crescent rolls

⅓ cup ranch dressing, plus more for dipping

8 slices Colby-Jack cheese (shredded is fine)

QUICK!

Rotisserie chicken makes this meal even quicker!

This is one of the most popular recipes I have ever made. Why is it so popular? It includes bacon and ranch, which we already know everyone goes crazy for, but then I wrap that up in another super popular ingredient: crescent rolls. So that's bacon, ranch, chicken, cheese, crescent rolls—all the good stuff made into one melty, flaky roll-up that everyone loves. These make an awesome quick dinner that you can serve with a side salad or some mac and cheese, and it will quickly become one of your go-tos.

1. Preheat your oven to 375°F. Grease a cookie sheet.

2. Heat a large skillet on medium-high heat with oil or butter. Place the chicken in the pan and season it with salt and pepper to taste. Cook the chicken for about 5 minutes, then flip it over and cook the other side until it is cooked through. This should take about 3 to 5 minutes per side.

3. Fry up your bacon, or microwave it if you choose.

4. Unroll the crescent roll dough or crescent rolls. If using crescent rolls, press the seams of two rolls together to make a rectangle. Repeat until you have 8 rectangles. If using dough, cut unrolled dough into 8 rectangles.

5. Place about 2 teaspoons of ranch on each dough rectangle. Add a slice of Colby-Jack cheese (torn to fit). Add 2 slices of bacon and one chicken strip.

6. Roll these up and place them seam-side down on the prepared cookie sheet.

7. Bake for 15 to 20 minutes, or until they are golden.

8. Serve the roll-ups with extra ranch for dipping.

ENCHILADA STUFFED SHELLS

Serves 6 to 8

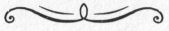

1 box large pasta shells

1 pound hamburger

One 1-ounce packet taco seasoning

One 15-ounce can refried beans

8 ounces shredded Colby-Jack cheese

8 ounces shredded Pepper Jack cheese

2 cans enchilada sauce

Scallions, chopped, for garnish

Yes, I have another mixed-up recipe. This one takes delicious enchilada filling and stuffs it into pasta shells before covering them in enchilada sauce and cheese. I created this recipe because my mom loves enchiladas but isn't the biggest fan of tortillas. Best of all, it is super simple and a great way to switch up the same old boring dinner. Moms, friends, kids—everyone loves it!

1. Preheat your oven to 350°F.

2. Bring a large pot of salted water to a boil. Boil the pasta according to the directions on the box. Drain the cooked pasta and let it cool.

3. Meanwhile, in a large skillet, brown the hamburger, draining off excess grease. Season with taco seasoning. Add the refried beans and half of each type of cheese.

4. Spread a little enchilada sauce across the bottom of a 9-by-13-inch dish.

5. Spoon the meat filling into the cooled shells and place them in the baking dish.

6. Cover the shells with the remaining enchilada sauce and cheese.

7. Bake, covered, for 30 minutes until bubbly.

8. Top with chopped scallions and serve.

TIP: This dish freezes beautifully!

CHICKEN PARM CUPS

Serves 4

1 bag frozen popcorn chicken (about 1½ to 2 cups)

One 8-ounce can crescent roll dough or one 8-count can crescent rolls

½ cup of your favorite marinara/ spaghetti sauce

2 cups shredded or fresh mozzarella cheese

Grated Parmesan cheese

Marinara sauce or ranch dressing, for serving

QUICK!

Popcorn chicken and canned biscuits help get this family favorite on the table in no time!

Chicken parm is a classic, right? But let's face it, it can be a little boring—delicious, yes, but boring. These little cups are amazing. They solve the boring problem and they come together in minutes with some help from the store. Dean loves them and I love that I can have dinner on the table in minutes.

1. Preheat your oven to 350°F. Grease a muffin tin.

2. Place the popcorn chicken on a baking sheet and bake for 13 to 15 minutes (or according to package directions).

3. Unroll the crescent roll dough or crescent rolls. If using crescent rolls, press the seams together to make one big rectangle. Cut the dough into 12 squares. Place a square in each well of your muffin tin.

4. Chop up your chicken and toss with ½ cup of the sauce.

5. Spoon the chicken into each crescent cup. Top each cup with the mozzarella and sprinkle with Parmesan cheese.

6. Bake for 12 to 15 minutes until melted and golden brown.

7. Serve with extra marinara sauce or ranch for dipping.

COPYCAT MEXICAN MELTS

Serves 4

1 pound ground beef

One 1-ounce packet taco seasoning

8 ounces shredded Cheddar or Colby-Jack cheese

8 tortillas

8 ounces shredded Pepper Jack cheese

Pico de gallo or chunky salsa

Mexican food is my life, and while I love a good meal at a Mexican restaurant I hit up the drive-thru for tacos once a week (ain't no shame in my cheap taco-lovin' game). My grandma and I share a love of fast food "Meximelts"—cheesy, melty little wraps of deliciousness—and I can never get enough. But sometimes once a week just isn't enough, so of course I had to figure out how to make them myself. And yes, they are just as quick as hitting up the drive-thru. Plus, when I make them at home I can make as many as I want and hang out on my sofa bingeing on movies and cheesy, melty goodness.

1. In a medium skillet over medium-high heat, cook the ground beef and drain off any remaining grease. Season with taco seasoning.

2. Place some Cheddar cheese on each tortilla (these are supposed to be extra cheesy so fill 'em up). Spoon on some of the beef filling. Top with shredded Pepper Jack. Spoon on a little salsa.

3. Roll each tortilla up and wrap them in paper towels.

4. Microwave 2 melts at a time for 1 minute.

5. Serve and enjoy!

TIP: These freeze well, so you can fill your freezer (I know I do).

COPYCAT MEXICAN PIZZAS

Serves 4

1 pound ground beef

One 1-ounce packet taco seasoning

¼ cup water

8 tostada or taco bowl shells (found in the refrigerated Mexican section of the store)

One 15-ounce can refried beans

4 tablespoons taco sauce

2 cups shredded Colby-Jack cheese

Choice of tomatoes, sour cream, scallions, for serving

Here I have another copycat recipe from my favorite drive-thru. This one is my mom's favorite and one of mine (I pretty much love everything there), and again I wanted to re-create it at home to hopefully cut down on my trips through the fast food line. These come together quick and when you make them at home, you cut down on the risk that all the cheese will end up on one side of your pizza.

1. Preheat your oven to 350°F.

2. In a medium skillet over medium-high heat, cook the ground beef and drain off any remaining grease.

3. Add the taco seasoning and ¼ cup water to the ground beef and cook for 3 more minutes.

4. Bake the taco bowl shells flat in the oven until they are just golden brown, about 5 minutes (keep your eye on them, they burn fast).

5. Preheat your broiler.

6. Spread 4 of the shells with refried beans. Split the ground beef between the 4 shells. Top each with the remaining shells. Spread 1 tablespoon of taco sauce on the top of each one. Top with the cheese.

7. Lightly broil the pizzas until the cheese is just melted.

8. Finish with your favorite toppings and enjoy!

TIP: You can find flat taco bowl shells in the refrigerated Mexican section of the grocery store.

LASAGNA PIZZA

Serves 4

There are some days when you just need carbs. Carbs on top of carbs, covered in cheese, can fix anything. Lasagna is super warm and comforting, but not always the fastest dinner to make. Pizza is always a hit and comes together much more quickly, so it just made sense to introduce these two so they could make the cheesiest, most delicious baby—lasagna pizza. Pasta and ricotta give this pizza its lasagna flavor, while it gets ground sausage and a premade crust from the pizza side of the family.

1 cup radiatore pasta

1 cup plus 3 tablespoons your favorite pizza or pasta sauce

1 premade pizza crust

2 tablespoons melted butter

1 teaspoon garlic salt (optional)

7 to 8 ounces ricotta cheese

2 cups shredded mozzarella cheese

½ pound Italian sausage, browned and crumbled

Grated parmesan cheese

1. Preheat your oven to 350°F.

2. Bring a pot of salted water to a boil. Cook the pasta according to the box directions and drain.

3. Mix the cooked pasta with 3 tablespoons of sauce. Spread the pizza crust with melted butter and a sprinkle of garlic salt, if using. Spread the ricotta all over the crust. Top with a layer of sauce followed by the mozzarella, cooked sausage, and pasta. Sprinkle with Parmesan.

4. Bake for 12 to 15 minutes until the cheese is bubbly and melted.

5. Cool slightly, slice, and serve to your hungry family!

QUICK!

Premade pizza crusts are a lifesaver. You can get them already baked, in a can, or a ball of dough to roll out yourself—they all make dinner quick and easy.

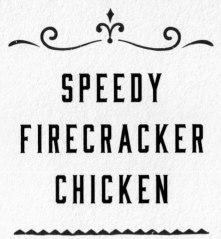

SPEEDY FIRECRACKER CHICKEN

Serves 4 to 6

1½ to 2 pounds frozen popcorn chicken

⅓ cup hot sauce (I use Frank's brand for hot wings since it is thicker than others)

1 cup packed light brown sugar

1 tablespoon water

1 teaspoons vinegar

Cooked rice, for serving

If there is one dish my whole family, my friends, my extended family, anyone I have ever known, wants me to cook on a daily basis, it is Firecracker Chicken. This dish, made of crispy fried chicken bites coated in a sweet and sticky sauce that gets ladled over fluffy white rice, is recipe perfection. It is also a pain in the butt to make. See, when I make it everyone wants it, and I mean *everyone,* so I have to make a lot, and it's a pretty laborious recipe no matter how many people you make it for. So I wised up and bought frozen pop-corn chicken and cut out the hard stuff. Now I just bake up the chicken nuggets while I reduce the sauce, then combine the two and dinner is done! I still make it the old-fashioned way for my mom's birthday, but other than that, I do this speedy version and save myself a ton of time (and grease-splatter burns).

1. Preheat your oven to 350°F.

2. Place the popcorn chicken on a cookie sheet and bake for 15 to 20 minutes, until crispy.

3. Mix the remaining ingredients together in a small saucepan and bring the mixture to a boil. Reduce the heat to a simmer and let the sauce reduce and thicken, 10 to 15 minutes, stirring frequently.

4. Pour the sauce over the chicken.

5. Serve over rice.

TIP: You can cut back on the amount of hot sauce to make it less spicy or sub in pineapple juice for some of the hot sauce.

MEATBALL SUB BUBBLE UP BAKE

Serves 4 to 6

One 8-count can large biscuits

1¾ cups spaghetti sauce

2 cups frozen meatballs

1½ cups shredded mozzarella cheese

By this time I feel we have gotten to know each other a litter better, right? You probably know that two of my favorite supermarket shortcuts are frozen meatballs and canned biscuits. So you knew that I would inevitably put them together. This super-fast recipe uses just 4 ingredients and one pan. It is amazing, it is hearty, it is comforting, it is what's for dinner tonight.

1. Preheat your oven to 375°F. Grease a 9-by-13-inch baking dish or 12-inch cast-iron skillet.

2. Cut each uncooked biscuit into 8 pieces. Mix the cut biscuits with the sauce and place the mixture in the baking dish. Place the meatballs on top of the biscuits and sprinkle with the cheese.

3. Bake, covered with foil, for about 35 minutes.

4. Remove the foil and bake for 5 more minutes.

TIP: For extra flavor, add in some frozen peppers and onions.

CHICKEN FAJITA QUESADILLAS

Serves 4

1½ cups frozen onion and pepper mix

1 tablespoon butter

1½ pounds boneless, skinless chicken breasts

One 1-ounce packet taco seasoning

8 flour tortillas

1 cup shredded Pepper Jack cheese

1 cup shredded Colby-Jack cheese

Sour cream, for serving

TIP: Make sure you put cheese on the bottom of your quesadilla and on top of the ingredients before putting the top tortilla on to make sure everything sticks together.

I love quesadillas. They are so warm and inviting and nonjudgmental. Think about it: quesadillas are super accepting and get along with any ingredient. Open your fridge and almost anything you find you can put inside. Quesadillas are one of my go-to dinners because, instead of making five different dinners for all my picky eaters, I can just make five different quesadillas. While my son likes his with just cheese and my sister likes hers with cheese and chicken, I love to make these chicken fajita quesadillas for the rest of us. Taco-seasoned chicken, sautéed onions and peppers, Colby-Jack and Pepper Jack all get down and dirty and melty in between two tortillas.

1. Sauté the veggies with butter in a large skillet until they are caramelized.

2. Meanwhile, cut the chicken into small slices and sprinkle with the taco seasoning.

3. Remove the veggies from the skillet and add in the chicken, cooking on medium heat until it is cooked through. Add the veggies to the chicken.

4. Place a clean, medium skillet on medium-high heat and spray it with cooking spray.

5. Place a tortilla down in the pan. Sprinkle ¼ of the Pepper Jack on the tortilla. Place some of the chicken/veggie mixture on top of that. Sprinkle ¼ of the Colby on top of that. Top the whole thing with another tortilla and give the top of the tortilla a spray with the cooking spray.

6. Check the bottom of the quesadilla and flip when it is browned. Remove the quesadilla from the pan when the second side is browned.

7. Repeat with the remaining tortillas.

8. Let the quesadillas cool slightly and then cut each one into four wedges with a pizza cutter. Serve with sour cream.

SLOW COOKER BEEF TIPS

Serves 6

1 can cream of onion soup

1 can cream of mushroom soup

3 pounds stew beef

1 cup frozen or canned vegetables (optional)

As soon as the weather dips down one degree below 80, as soon as the first leaf drops from the tree, as soon as the morning air is just a bit cooler, I am busting out all my fall stuff. Scarves and quilts, pumpkins and apple cider—I am ready! That also means I am pulling out my slow cooker for some of those hearty, comforting, warm meals that are perfect for the cooler weather.

These slow cooker beef tips are one of my favorite slow cooker meals because it only uses four ingredients and the flavor is out of this world. Now, I would assume that if canned products and such offend you, you are probably gone by now. If so, shield yourself from this recipe, because we are going to get down and dirty with some canned cream soups in a super vintage dish. Trust me, the canned soup is what makes this dish.

Four ingredients is all you need to make tender, flavorful beef tips that melt in your mouth and create their own gravy that can be ladled over rice, noodles, mashed potatoes, a shoe, anything.

1. Mix the two soups in the bottom of your crockpot, add the beef, and stir.

2. Cover and let the stew cook on low for 6 to 8 hours or on high for 4 to 6 hours.

3. One hour before serving, throw in your frozen peas, carrots, or any other frozen veggies, if you wish. If you are using canned or cooked veggies, add them 20 minutes before serving.

4. Serve over rice, noodles, or potatoes.

TIP: You can add carrots and peas to this dish to make it more like a stew.

PORK EGG ROLL BOWL

Serves 4

Being Southern, I of course have an affinity for all things fried—fried chicken, fried pickles, fried fish, fried shrimp, fried hushpuppies, fried steak, fried turkey—and when we order Chinese takeout, I always make sure to double up on the egg rolls. After all, they're the best part of takeout, right? I usually eat them a few hours later when I'm hungry again. I wanted to re-create takeout pork egg rolls at home, but, *ugh*, frying—no thanks! I hate frying food. I stink, my house stinks, I get grease-splatter burns, my kitchen becomes one big grease slick—you can practically skate on the floor. I avoid it whenever I can. So, I figured out how to get all that yummy egg roll flavor without the frying by making these pork egg roll bowls.

2 cups uncooked white rice

4 cups water

1 pound ground pork

3 to 4 garlic cloves, minced

5 scallions, chopped

1 bag shredded coleslaw mix

3 tablespoons low-sodium soy sauce

3 tablespoons brown sugar

Black pepper

Crispy wonton strips, chopped scallions, and sweet and sour duck sauce, for serving (optional)

1. Add the rice and the water to a pot and bring it to a boil, then cover and reduce the heat to low for 16 minutes.

2. Brown the pork with the garlic and scallions in a large skillet over medium-high heat.

3. Add in the coleslaw mix, soy, and brown sugar. Season with pepper. Cook until the cabbage is cooked down and almost caramelized.

4. Serve the pork over the rice and top with crispy wontons, scallions, and duck sauce if desired.

TIP: Crispy wonton strips and a drizzle of duck sauce bring this dish together.

ONE-POT CHICKEN BACON RANCH PASTA

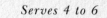

Serves 4 to 6

1 pound bacon, chopped

1 pound boneless, skinless chicken breast, diced

1 garlic clove

2 cups chicken stock

½ cup milk

4 tablespoons ranch dressing (plus more for topping if desired)

8 ounces short pasta

1 cup plus ¼ cup shredded Colby-Jack cheese

Guys! I got more bacon and ranch for you, this time with pasta! (And all in one pot.)

One-pot dinners are a lifesaver; they cook up quick, and, if you're like me and hate doing the dishes, you'll love only having one pot to wash out. You need this pot of warm, comforting, cheesy, bacony, ranchy goodness in your life right now.

1. Brown the bacon in a large pot. Remove the bacon from the pot and drain on paper towels. Remove all but 1 tablespoon of the grease from the pot.

2. Add the diced chicken to the pot and season it with salt and pepper. Begin browning the chicken and add in one clove of garlic. The chicken does not have to cook all the way through here.

3. Add 2 cups chicken stock, ½ cup milk, 4 tablespoons ranch dressing, and the pasta. Stir this mixture and bring it to a boil.

4. Turn the heat to low and cook, covered, for 20 minutes.

5. Remove the pot from the heat and stir in 1 cup shredded cheese. Top with the bacon and ¼ cup additional cheese.

TIP: Add hot sauce for a buffalo wing spin!

SLOW COOKER CARAMELIZED PORK TACOS

Serves 6 to 8

There is nothing I love more in this world than tacos. Maybe my kids, but that's pushing it. Plus, my kids don't come with cheese. I love all tacos: soft tacos, hard tacos, short tacos, fat tacos, any tacos. I would call these caramelized pork tacos my version of carnitas, but people take their carnitas very seriously and I don't want 1,000 angry emails telling me these aren't carnitas, so these are just pork tacos. What I can say for sure, though, is that these are super-duper easy. You just throw a few ingredients into your slow cooker and by the end of the day you will have swoon-worthy tacos. A quick trip under the broiler caramelizes them, and then I put them on tortillas with my Mexican Restaurant White Dip (page 45) and some crispy fried onions. (Yes, the ones in the can; they aren't just for green bean casserole.)

One 2- to 3-pound pork loin roast

Two to three 1-ounce packets taco seasoning (1 per pound)

3 tablespoons brown sugar

1 tablespoon garlic salt

Black pepper

3 cups water

Crunchy fried onions (the kind in a can or bag)

Tortillas

Mexican Restaurant White Dip (page 45)

1. Place the pork roast, taco seasoning, sugar, and garlic salt in a 6-quart slow cooker and sprinkle the roast with pepper. Add the water. Cook on high for 4 to 6 hours, or low for 6 to 8 hours.

2. When the pork is tender, preheat your broiler. Line a baking sheet with foil.

3. Remove the pork from the slow cooker and shred it. Place the shredded pork on the prepared baking sheet. Spoon about 1 cup of cooking liquid over the pork.

4. Place the pork under the broiler until it becomes caramelized, about 5 minutes depending on your broiler.

5. Place the shredded pork on a warmed tortilla, top with crunchy onions, and drizzle with the white dip.

TIP: These tacos are so flavorful they don't need cheese (I can't believe I'm saying that), but the sauce and onions are a must.

SOUTHERN FRIED CABBAGE WITH BACON AND NOODLES

Serves 4 to 6

Wanna know how I get my picky eaters to try veggies? Bacon! Bacon is the Band-Aid of the food world. Bacon can fix any recipe and get anyone to eat anything. Bacon is how I got my mom and sister to love cabbage—well, that and by mixing it with caramelized onions, egg noodles, and *buttah*! This has become one of our favorite dinners and you can make it more hearty by adding smoked sausage or chicken.

1 pound bacon, diced

1 onion, thinly sliced

One 16-ounce bag shredded coleslaw mix

1 pound egg noodles

2 tablespoons butter

Black pepper

1. Fry the diced bacon in a large skillet until it is crisp. Drain the bacon on a paper towel and place it in a large bowl. Drain all but 3 to 4 tablespoons of the bacon grease.

2. Add the thinly sliced onion to the bacon grease in the skillet and cook until it is caramelized. Add the onions to the bacon in your bowl.

3. Meanwhile, bring a pot of salted water to a boil and cook the egg noodles according to their package directions, then drain them.

4. Add the cabbage to the skillet and cook until it is tender.

5. Add the cabbage, egg noodles, and butter to the bowl with the onions and bacon. Add in a little black pepper to taste, then toss and serve!

Don't waste time chopping cabbage, just buy a bag of coleslaw mix.

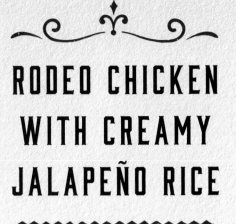

RODEO CHICKEN WITH CREAMY JALAPEÑO RICE

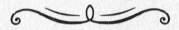

Serves 4 to 6

I know I talk about how much I love Mexican food and you would probably assume I go to all the Mexican joints as far as the eye can see. I don't, I go to one only (aside from Taco Bell of course). There is this little Mexican restaurant, your typical hole-in-the-wall, not-fancy place that always ends up having the absolute best food. They make an amazing chicken dish with onions and cheese sauce and they serve it with fries that also get smothered in cheese. It's my absolute favorite, and it's all I order—and the same goes for my mom, and my grandma, and everyone I know. While I could never replicate it at home, I sure do try, and the outcome is fabulous!

For the chicken

1 tablespoon butter

1 onion, thinly sliced

4 boneless, skinless chicken breasts

One 1-ounce package taco seasoning

One 16-ounce container refrigerated white queso dip (such as Gordo's)

Tortillas

For the rice

1½ cups uncooked rice

3 cups water

2 cups shredded Pepper Jack cheese

One 4-ounce can diced green chilies

½ cup sour cream

One 10-ounce can cream of chicken soup

Salt and black pepper

TIP: I also serve this on tortillas with that multipurpose, super delicious Mexican Restaurant White Dip (page 45).

Make the chicken:

1. Melt the butter in a large skillet and add in the thinly sliced onion. Cook over medium heat until the onions are caramelized, 10 to 15 minutes, then remove the onions from the pan.

2. Season both sides of the chicken with the taco seasoning and place it in the skillet over medium heat. Cook 3 to 5 minutes on each side until the chicken is cooked through. Add the onions on top of the chicken and reduce the heat to low.

3. Microwave the queso for 1 minute (or according to package instructions) and pour over the chicken in the skillet. Cover with the lid and simmer for 5 to 10 minutes.

Make the rice:

4. Bring the rice and water to a boil, cover, and reduce the heat to low. Cook for 16 minutes.

5. Add the cheese, chilies, sour cream, cream of chicken soup, and salt and pepper to taste to the rice. Let this mixture cook on low for 7 to 10 minutes.

6. Serve the whole meal together for a fabulous dinner!

QUESO CHICKEN BURRITOS

Serves 4

1 tablespoon butter

1 cup of frozen mixed onions and peppers

4 boneless, skinless chicken breasts, cut into bite-sized pieces

One 1-ounce packet fajita seasoning

4 flour tortillas

One 16-ounce container refrigerated white queso dip (such as Gordo's)

Store-bought queso makes re-creating these burritos at home easy.

For more than 20 years I have ordered the same exact thing every time I hit up my favorite restaurant (see previous recipe). One day, I was feeling a little crazy—maybe it was the holiday season or maybe I just wanted something to distract me from the two carts full of things I just bought at Target—but I ordered something different, the lunch special nonetheless. And you know what happened? It started a chain reaction. My mom, my grandma, my uncle all followed suit. Then you know what happened? We had an amazing meal!

To make these burritos, chicken is sautéed with onions and peppers and stuffed into a tortilla, rolled up, and then smothered in queso. I could have eaten 12!

1. Heat a large skillet over medium-high heat and add the butter. Add the peppers and onions and let them cook down until the onions become translucent.

2. Add the chicken to the skillet and brown for 8 to 10 minutes or until it's cooked through.

3. Microwave the cheese dip for 1 minute (or according to package directions).

4. Evenly distribute the chicken filling among your tortillas.

5. Roll the tortillas up and spoon a good amount of queso dip over each one. Serve!

TIP: This would be equally delicious with steak!

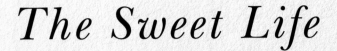

The Sweet Life

SALTED CARAMEL BROWNIE TRIFLES

KEY LIME PIE DIP

CHOCOLATE SILK PIE DIP

BANANA SPLIT CAKE

TIRAMISU POKE CAKE

CREAMY RASPBERRY FREEZE PIE

ORANGE CREAMSICLE PIE

CHOCOLATE CUPCAKE MILK SHAKE

BOSTON CREAM PIE TRIFLES

NO-BAKE FLUFFERNUTTER COOKIES

PEANUT BUTTER EXPLOSION CAKE

CINNAMON "FRIED" CARAMEL ICE CREAM

LEMON-GLAZED CAKE BITES

CARAMEL ICE CREAM SANDWICH CAKE

CHOCOLATE-COVERED MARSHMALLOW CHERRY POPS

LEMON CHEESECAKE COOKIE POPS

PEANUT BUTTER COOKIE POPS

S'MORES RICE CRISPY CAKE

BANANA SPLIT CHEESECAKE COOKIE BITES

PIG PICKIN' TRES LECHES CAKES

SALTED CARAMEL BROWNIE TRIFLES

Serves 4

One 3-ounce box caramel instant
  pudding

1½ cups milk

4 cups brownie crumbles

2 cups Cool Whip

Hot fudge

Salted caramel ice cream topping

Chocolate caramel candies, for
  topping

Flaky sea salt, for topping
  (optional)

You might expect that as a food blogger I know how to make a decent brownie, right? *Wrong.* While I do have some successes, most of the time I end up with a delicious mess that won't come out of the pan, or I try to avoid that and end up over-baking them. But I am okay with that, because those less-than-perfect brownies get their ugly duckling ending in these decadent trifles. These are so good you might start messing up brownies on purpose!

The mason jar trend may be dwindling down, but I am still in love with mine. I use them for everything from décor to drinking. The best way to use them, however, is to fill them to the brim with these Salted Caramel Brownie Trifles.

1. Mix the pudding and milk until they are combined and chill 5 minutes to set.

2. Add about ¼ cup of the crumbled brownie to each of 4 mason jars. Spoon in ¼ cup of the pudding. Next add ¼ cup Cool Whip. Then drizzle in a little hot fudge and caramel.

3. Repeat the layers one more time. You want the last layer to be Cool Whip, then the drizzles.

4. Top with caramel candy and a pinch of sea salt and serve!

TIP: Some people love walnuts in their brownies, some don't. If you feel like a nut, feel free to sprinkle some in. For another variation on this recipe, simply swap the caramel pudding for butterscotch pudding.

KEY LIME PIE DIP

Serves 4 to 6

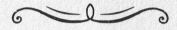

For the dip

1 cup fresh key lime or lime juice

Two 14-ounce cans sweetened
  condensed milk

Whipped cream or Cool Whip,
  for serving

Piecrust Dippers (below), graham
  crackers, or vanilla wafers, for
  serving

For the Piecrust Dippers (optional)

1 premade refrigerated pie
  dough

1 tablespoon granulated sugar

TIP: You can also serve this as a dip
for fruit. Pretty much anything is going
to taste good with it.

My husband loves key lime pie. Sometimes, when I'm feeling super domestic, I whip up one from scratch. But I wanted something easier and the Key Lime Pie Dip I ended up creating is ridiculously fast, incredibly easy, and of course delicious. This dip is perfect for summer (but that doesn't mean you can't snack on this during a snowstorm). Now I can look like a domestic goddess and satisfy my husband's pie craving in just minutes!

I know this is a book on shortcuts and I know you're thinking that bottled lime juice would make this recipe even quicker, but don't go there. Don't do it. The dip needs the fresh lime juice to set up. However, I will not stop you from using regular limes instead of key limes (those things are tiny and hard to juice!).

Make the dip:
1. Combine the lime juice with the condensed milk. Spread in a pie dish.
2. Refrigerate for at least 2 hours.
3. Top with the whipped cream.
4. Serve with graham crackers, vanilla wafers, or these easy piecrust dippers.

Make the Piecrust Dippers:
5. Preheat your oven to 350°F.
6. Unroll the pie dough. Cut it into strip, triangles, or whatever shape floats your boat.
7. Place the shapes on a baking sheet and sprinkle just a touch of sugar over them.
8. Bake for 8 to 10 minutes, until golden (watch closely so they do not burn).
9. Cool completely and serve with the Key Lime Pie Dip.

CHOCOLATE SILK PIE DIP

Serves 4 to 6

There is no one in my family who would turn down Chocolate Silk Pie. It is such a favorite that it makes an appearance at every holiday—Easter, Thanksgiving, Christmas Eve, Halloween, Presidents' Day. Having had such success with my Key Lime Pie Dip, I of course wanted to turn all kinds of pie into dips. I decided to start with this family favorite. I mean, does it get any better than chocolate pie you can dip stuff into? Well, maybe a trip to Target sans kids, but other than that, no.

2 cups milk

One 5.1-ounce box chocolate instant pudding

4 cups Cool Whip

1 bar chocolate

Piecrust Dippers (page 191), graham crackers, or vanilla wafers, for serving

1. In a mixing bowl, beat the milk and pudding mix until they are combined. Whip in 2 cups of Cool Whip.

2. Pour the mixture into a pie plate and refrigerate for 2 hours.

3. Create chocolate curls by using a vegetable peeler on a bar of chocolate.

4. Top the dip with extra Cool Whip and chocolate curls.

5. Serve with piecrust dippers, graham crackers, or vanilla wafers.

TIP: This is also fabulous as a dip for fruit, and of course, if you want to go old school, just pop it in a piecrust and *voilà*, pie!

BANANA SPLIT CAKE

Serves 8 to 12

1 store-bought angel food cake

Two 3-ounce boxes banana instant pudding

3 cups milk

One 12-ounce jar hot fudge

Rainbow sprinkles

Whipped cream

8 to 10 maraschino cherries with stems

QUICK!

The bakery is your friend here, mama, and premade angel food cake your hero. I mean, technically this cake is homemade, just not all parts of it.

Dean is in school now, and that means bake sales. While I am all for getting down and dirty with my mixer and whipping up some homemade treats, there are times when I'm just a hot mom mess and forget. That's when this cake saves the day. It looks amazing, like it took you all day long to make. The perfectly drippy hot fudge, layers of fluffy angel food cake, and creamy banana pudding will have the PTA bowing at your feet. And you know what? This cake takes minutes to make; just minutes, people!

1. Slice the angel food cake horizontally into 3 slices.

2. Mix the banana pudding with the milk and whisk until it starts to thicken.

3. Spoon half of the pudding onto the bottom cake layer. Place the middle cake layer on top of the pudding. Place the rest of the pudding on top of the middle layer. Place the top layer on top of the cake.

4. Pour on the hot fudge, spooning it evenly across the top of the cake and letting it drip off the edges.

5. Decorate with sprinkles, whipped cream, and cherries.

6. Refrigerate to firm up for at least 2 hours.

7. Slice and serve!

TIP: This cake would be fabulous with nuts sprinkled on top.

TIRAMISU POKE CAKE

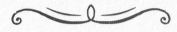

Serves 8 to 12

One 15-ounce box yellow or white cake mix

3 eggs (or amount indicated on cake mix instructions)

1 cup of water (or amount indicated on cake mix instructions)

⅓ cup vegetable oil (or amount indicated on cake mix instructions)

1 cup brewed coffee

½ cup granulated sugar, divided in half

One 3.4-ounce box vanilla instant pudding

2 cups cold milk

One 8-ounce block cream cheese, softened

4 cups whipped cream or Cool Whip

Cocoa powder

Back when I first started blogging, poke cakes became insanely popular. They were everywhere! I decided I needed to get me some of that action and came up with this Tiramisu Poke Cake. This amazing dessert has cream cheese, coffee, and chocolate. The best part is that it starts with a cake mix.

1. Preheat your oven to 350°F. Grease a 9-by-13-inch baking dish.

2. Mix the cake mix with the eggs, water, and oil, according to the box directions, and pour it into the prepared dish.

3. Bake the cake according to the box directions.

4. Cool the cake and poke it all over with the handle of a wooden spoon.

5. Mix 1 cup of brewed coffee with ¼ cup sugar and pour the mixture all over the cake.

6. Combine the pudding with the milk in a large bowl. Chill for 5 minutes to set.

7. Beat pudding with the remaining ¼ cup of sugar, cream cheese, and 2 cups of whipped cream until blended.

8. Spread the cream cheese mixture over the top of the cake. Cover the cake with the remaining 2 cups of whipped cream. Sprinkle with cocoa powder.

9. Chill for at least 4 hours and serve!

TIP: Poke cakes get better each day! If you have leftovers, be sure to refrigerate them.

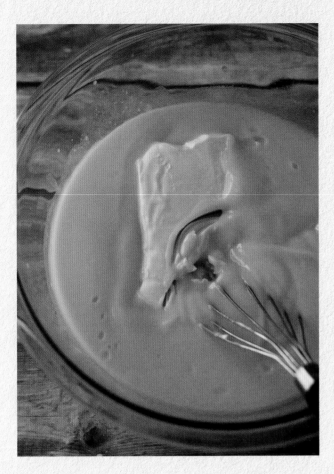

Poke cakes are super easy to make because you don't have to remove the cake from the pan, and, even if you over-bake your cake, poking it and soaking it keeps it moist. They're a foolproof way to get a deliciously creamy cake. You just choose your cake mix, bake it, poke holes in it, and then cover it with a creamy filling that sinks down into those holes, creating the most delicious dessert.

CREAMY RASPBERRY FREEZE PIE

Serves 6 to 8

One 8-ounce block cream cheese, softened

One 7-ounce jar marshmallow fluff

3 cups raspberry sherbet or sorbet, softened slightly

One 8-ounce container Cool Whip

1 piecrust, prebaked

Extra Cool Whip and fresh raspberries, for decorating (optional)

QUICK!

You don't even have to measure anything when it comes to this pie; it does not get any easier than that.

Okay y'all, if you have got an issue with Cool Whip (one of the loves of my life), flip the page now. For the rest of you, get ready for the best pie ever!

I love sherbet; it has always been my favorite ice cream. Move over cookies and cream; no thank you rocky road. For me it was always sherbet, the kind that is raspberry, lime, and orange all lined up in that cardboard box—yum! Maybe that's why this is my favorite pie, because it gets its flavor from sherbet. It doesn't get more vintage than this recipe. It's got sherbet, it's got Cool Whip, it's got cream cheese, it's got marshmallow fluff—this pie has got it going on! This recipe has been in my family all my life and probably longer. I love to make it for Easter because of its pretty pastel color, but we eat it all summer long.

1. In a mixing bowl, beat the cream cheese and marshmallow fluff with an electric mixer. Add the sherbet and mix until combined. Fold in the whipped topping.

2. Pour the mixture into the crust. Top with extra dollops of Cool Whip and raspberries if desired.

3. Freeze for 4 hours.

4. Slice and serve.

5. Store any leftover pie in the freezer.

TIP: Change up the flavor of the sherbet for a completely different pie—like the one on the next page.

ORANGE CREAMSICLE PIE

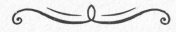

Serves 6 to 8

Remember that yummy raspberry freezer pie we just made? In that recipe, I mentioned that you could switch up the sherbet to make different types of pie. Well, I did some of the work for you with this Orange Creamsicle Pie.

Remember hitting up the ice cream truck and getting a creamsicle? That orangey outside giving way to the creamy center making it the perfect cool treat on a hot day? (P.S. Are anyone else's neighborhood ice cream trucks jerks? The one around here never stops, even when I'm waving cash!) My sister and grandma love, love, love creamsicle-flavored anything, so making this pie for them was a no-brainer.

One 8-ounce block cream cheese, softened

One 7-ounce jar marshmallow fluff

3 cups orange sherbet, softened slightly

One 8-ounce container Cool Whip

1 piecrust, prebaked

Extra Cool Whip and mandarin oranges, for decorating (optional)

1. In a mixing bowl, beat the cream cheese and marshmallow fluff with an electric mixer. Add the sherbet and mix until it is combined. Fold in the whipped topping.

2. Pour the mixture into the piecrust.

3. Top with extra dollops of Cool Whip and oranges if desired.

4. Freeze for 4 hours.

5. Slice and serve.

6. Store any leftover pie in the freezer.

TIP: Garnish with orange slices or mandarin oranges—or not, I'm not going to tell you how to live your life.

CHOCOLATE CUPCAKE MILK SHAKE

Serves 4

Cake and ice cream go together perfectly. Birthday party after birthday party you have that sweet combo. But you know what part I love best? When the ice cream starts to melt and kind of soaks into the cake, creating a delicious collision of both flavors and textures. Yeah, it's awesome. For quite some time my mom and I were hooked on eating store-bought pound cake and Nutty Buddy ice cream. I would put it all in one bowl and mix it all together. Trust me, it was heavenly. So I got the idea to make this concoction into a legit recipe—a milk shake! Super simple to prepare and sinfully scrumptious, this Chocolate Cupcake Milk Shake is amazing!

4 chocolate cupcakes (frosting and all!)

5 cups chocolate ice cream or birthday cake ice cream

3 cups chocolate milk or regular milk

Hot fudge, sprinkles, and whipped cream, for garnish

1. In a blender, add the cupcakes, ice cream, and milk. Blend together.

2. Pour some hot fudge into each of four glasses and swirl it around the inside. Then dip the rims of the glasses in hot fudge and sprinkles.

3. Pour the milk shake inside and serve!

NOTE: To make these shakes extra special, garnish each one with a whole mini cupcake!

QUICK!

You can use store-bought cupcakes or even stale cupcakes (if cupcakes ever last that long in your house).

BOSTON CREAM PIE TRIFLES

Serves 8

One 15-ounce box yellow cake mix

1 cup water (or amount indicated on cake mix directions)

3 eggs (or amount indicated on cake mix directions)

⅓ cup oil (or amount indicated on cake mix directions)

One 5-ounce box vanilla instant pudding

3 cups milk

Hot fudge topping

Cool Whip, for serving

8 Maraschino cherries, for garnish (optional)

I always felt like I was a little weird about dough-nuts when I was younger. All of the other kids were crazy for the pink ones with sprinkles, or choc-olate ones with sprinkles, or anything with sprinkles. Meanwhile, I was over there by my weird self ordering a Boston cream-filled doughnut. For quite some time I didn't even know there was a Boston cream pie, I just thought it was a doughnut thing—*d'oh!* Long story short, I love Boston cream pie stuff and I love trifles (and mason jars). These come together in no time and look just as scrumptious as they taste!

1. Preheat your oven to 350°F.

2. Mix the cake mix with the water, eggs, and oil, according to the box directions.

3. Bake the cake in a 9-by-13-inch baking dish according to the box directions.

4. Let the cake cool and then cut it into one-inch cubes.

5. Mix the pudding mix with the cold milk and whisk until combined, then chill for 5 minutes to set.

6. In small mason jars start layering the cake, pudding, and hot fudge.

7. When the jars are filled up, top off with Cool Whip. Finish them with a cherry on top!

TIP: I serve these as individual trifles but you can make one big one if you like!

NO-BAKE FLUFFERNUTTER COOKIES

Makes 3 dozen

6 cups cornflakes

1 cup mini marshmallows

1 cup granulated sugar

1 cup light corn syrup

1 cup creamy peanut butter

This recipe is super special to me and my family. It's an old recipe from an old church cookbook. We have made these cookies so many times the pages the recipe is on stick together from years of peanut-buttery fingers. When I was growing up, there was nothing more exciting than walking into the kitchen and seeing my mom dropping the cookie mix onto big sheets of wax paper that covered the table. Waiting for these to set was torture, but so worth it. When they were done, we would wrap them up individually and snack on them all week. I could eat these every day and never get tired of them.

These cookies are superfast to make and perfect when you want a sweet treat without turning on the oven. The original recipe called for peanuts, but I subbed those out for mini marshmallows to get a fluffernutter thing going on.

1. Place the cornflakes and marshmallows in a large bowl.

2. Combine the sugar and corn syrup in a nonstick pot over medium-low heat. When the sugar has dissolved add the peanut butter, stirring to combine.

3. Pour the peanut butter mixture over the cornflakes and stir to combine.

4. Quickly drop heaping tablespoonfuls of the batter onto wax paper.

5. Let the cookies cool and set for about 30 minutes. Store in an airtight container.

TIP: If you want a little more crunch, add a handful or two of salted peanuts.

PEANUT BUTTER EXPLOSION CAKE

Serves 8 to 12

One 15-ounce box devil's food cake mix

1 cup of water (or amount indicated on cake mix instructions)

3 eggs (or amount indicated on cake mix instructions)

⅓ cup vegetable oil (or amount indicated on cake mix instructions)

1 cup plus ½ cup peanut butter

⅓ cup powdered sugar

4 tablespoons (½ stick) butter, melted

½ cup hot fudge

1 cup mini peanut butter cups

TIP: My only tip for you is don't skimp on the hot fudge; never skimp on fudge.

For Dean's bake sale this year I felt like I needed to pull out all the stops. He was in kindergarten, it was our first bake sale, and I wanted to show off my stuff. I wanted to make something that everyone would want. You know what everyone loves? Chocolate and peanut butter. (You can put Reese's Cups on anything and people will flip.) So, I pulled out my trusty chocolate cake mix, made a peanut butter filling, and baked it up in a Bundt pan. Then, just to really amp it up, I drizzled hot fudge and peanut butter all over that bad boy. Last but not least—because it still wasn't quite over-the-top enough—I chopped up some Reese's and covered it in them. I delivered that cake to the gym for the sale and walked away like a boss! I knew I had a winner on my hands, and now you too can create this masterpiece.

1. Preheat your oven to 350°F. Grease a Bundt pan.

2. Prepare the cake mix with the water, eggs, and oil, according to the box directions. Pour half of the cake batter into the Bundt pan.

3. Mix 1 cup of peanut butter with the powdered sugar and the butter. Spoon the peanut butter filling in a ring into the pan. Pour the rest of the cake mix on top of the peanut butter ring.

4. Bake the cake for 40 to 45 minutes.

5. Let the cake cool for 10 minutes. Run a knife around the edge of the pan. Let the cake cool 15 minutes more. Remove the cake from the pan and onto a cake rack to let it cool completely.

6. Warm up the hot fudge in a microwave-safe bowl and drizzle it over the cake.

7. In a microwave-safe bowl, heat up ½ cup peanut butter and drizzle it over the cake.

8. Chop half the peanut butter cups and leave the other half whole, and sprinkle them all over cake.

CINNAMON "FRIED" CARAMEL ICE CREAM

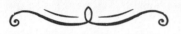

Serves 8

4 cups caramel ice cream

2 cups crushed cinnamon toast cereal

Caramel sauce, to serve

One day I decided I would try to make fried ice cream, to see what it was all about. We've already talked about my aversion to frying, and I was not about to drop some ice cream in the deep fryer and hope for the best! So I faked it, and it was the best decision I could have made. Just because we're not frying this doesn't mean it comes without a mess, but the outcome is oh-so worth it! Balls of ice cream are rolled in crushed-up cinnamon sugar cereal (the best cereal ever made), and then a caramel drizzle tops the whole thing off, creating an over-the-top dessert that is ready in minutes.

1. Scoop out eight ½-cup scoops of ice cream that are about 1 cup each in size. Roll the ice cream into 8 balls. Place the balls on a cookie sheet and pop them in the freezer until they firm back up a little.

2. Crush up the cereal finely and spread it out in a baking dish or other rimmed dish.

3. Pull the ice cream out of the freezer and roll the ice cream scoops in the cereal, forming them into balls as you go. Place the first cereal-coated ice cream ball on another tray and put it back in the freezer while you repeat the steps with the other scoops.

4. When all the scoops are coated and back in the freezer, let them freeze back up for 2 to 4 hours.

5. Serve with a drizzle of caramel sauce on top!

TIP: Cinnamon not your thing? Just crush up whatever cereal you watch your Saturday morning cartoons with.

LEMON-GLAZED CAKE BITES

Makes 4 dozen

I love lemon desserts. It started on the 4th of July: I was 5 years old, standing in the street in my striped bathing suit, ponytail dripping down my back, staring at the fireworks in the sky, when my grandma brought out lemon bars. They were tart and sweet, and as the powdered sugar coated my lips I fell in love with lemon.

Glazed Cake Bites—I make them a million ways—are adorable and so easy to make, and I love a good glaze. So it should be no big surprise that my favorite way to make them is lemon. They're just *so* light and refreshing, and the glaze keeps them moist for days (not that they will stick around that long).

For the cake bites

1 box lemon cake mix

1 cup water (or amount indicated on cake mix directions)

3 eggs (or amount indicated on cake mix directions)

⅓ cup oil (or amount indicated on cake mix directions)

For the glaze

2 pounds powdered sugar

½ cup water

½ cup corn syrup

2 to 3 teaspoons lemon juice

Poppy seeds

TIP: These make a perfect dessert or snack, but are also fabulous at a brunch.

Make the cake bites:

1. Preheat your oven to 375°F. Lightly grease a 48-well mini muffin tin. (You can bake these in 2 batches if you only have one pan.)

2. Mix the cake mix according to the box directions. Divide the batter evenly among the muffin wells (about half full).

3. Bake for 10 to 13 minutes.

4. Cool for 5 minutes. Remove the cakes from the muffin wells to a cooling rack and let them cool completely.

Make the glaze:

5. Place wax paper under your cooling rack to catch drips.

6. In a medium saucepan, mix all the glaze ingredients. Heat over low heat, stirring frequently, until the sugar is dissolved, then remove from the heat.

7. Dip a cake into the glaze, ensuring the whole cake gets coated in glaze. Place the cake topside down on the cooling rack. Sprinkle with poppy seeds immediately.

8. Repeat until all cakes are coated.

9. Let the cakes stand until the glaze is set, about 15 minutes.

CARAMEL ICE CREAM SANDWICH CAKE

Serves 8

While there are days that I love to pull out the mixer, preheat the oven, and just relax with some baking, there are also days when I just need something extra quick, or something that doesn't require baking. No-bake desserts are a busy mom's best friend. They are delish, and you look like Betty Crocker without even opening the oven. If you've got 5 minutes, you've got dessert!

9 ice cream sandwiches, unwrapped

1 cup hot fudge

One 8-ounce container Cool Whip

1 cup caramel sauce

1 package of Rolos

TIP: Switch up the flavor of the ice cream sandwiches for a different take on this easy treat.

1. Lay 3 ice cream sandwiches on a cake plate.
2. Smother the ice cream sandwiches in hot fudge (as much or as little as you like).
3. Top the hot fudge-slathered sandwiches with a layer of Cool Whip.
4. Drizzle caramel all over the top.
5. Make another layer of 3 ice cream sandwiches, then hot fudge, Cool Whip, and caramel. Repeat one more time.
6. Finish by making sure the whole cake is covered in Cool Whip and caramel. Sprinkle Rolos on top.
7. Place the cake in the freezer for at least 2 hours so everything can come together happily.
8. Let the cake sit out for 5 minutes before cutting.
9. Serve and watch it disappear in minutes.

CHOCOLATE-COVERED MARSHMALLOW CHERRY POPS

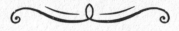

Makes 2 dozen

24 maraschino cherries with stems intact

1 pound melting chocolate, almond bark, or chocolate chips

Sprinkles

1 bag regular-sized marshmallows

24 paper straws

TIP: Use different colored chocolate to make these for any holiday.

Want to make a dessert kids will go crazy for? Pop marshmallows on a stick, cover them in chocolate, place a cherry and sprinkles on top, and watch kids go crazy! I originally made these one Christmas Eve because they looked so festive, but I didn't think anyone would really like them. Boy was I wrong: They were the first things to go! The chocolate cherry combo is just like those boxes of chocolate-covered cherries everyone gets/gives at Christmastime.

These marshmallow pops are so quick and easy, and the combination of flavors and textures makes for the perfect dessert. This is really a base recipe. You can get crazy with all the toppings you want—sprinkles, nuts, chocolate chips, anything goes!

1. Drain, rinse, and pat dry the cherries.
2. Get about 4 tall glasses ready to place the pops in to set up. They set pretty quickly so you can rotate the set ones out.
3. Microwave the chocolate in 30-second increments until it is completely melted.
4. Pour sprinkles into a shallow dish, such as a ramekin.
5. Stick a paper straw into the end of each marshmallow.
6. Dip marshmallows one at a time into the chocolate, shaking off the excess. Place the marshmallow in the dish of sprinkles and roll it around to coat.
7. Gently remove the marshmallow from the sprinkles and stand it up in a glass to harden. Repeat with the remaining marshmallows.
8. Dip a cherry halfway into the chocolate and place on top of a marshmallow. Repeat.
9. Let the cherries dry.
10. Serve!

LEMON CHEESECAKE COOKIE POPS

Makes 30

1 package lemon crème cookies

One 8-ounce block cream cheese, softened

1 pound white almond bark

30 paper straws

(QUICK!)

There are more and more flavors of sandwich cookies these days and each one makes a delicious cookie pop.

Have you noticed how cake pops are all the rage? Well, have you ever made them? There are a lot of steps involved . . . a lot! Then I found that you could make them with Oreos and cream cheese—and that's it. Between you and me, they are 1,000 times better than regular ol' cake pops (and easier, too). I have to make these cookie pops all the time, for so-and-so's birthday, for my sister's dance class, for Thanksgiving, because it's Wednesday. . . . These Lemon Cheesecake Cookie Pops are simple but real crowd-pleasers. I never have any left *(sigh)*.

1. Add all the cookies except two to a food processor and crush finely. Add the cream cheese to the cookies and blend until they are combined.

2. Roll the cookie mixture into 1-inch balls and place them on a wax paper-lined tray.

3. Place a paper straw in each ball.

4. Place the tray in the freezer for 1 hour or more.

5. Microwave the almond bark in 30-second increments until it is fully melted.

6. Remove the cookie balls from the freezer and dip them one by one into the almond bark, tapping off the excess. Place them back on the wax-lined tray.

7. Finely crush the two reserved cookies and sprinkle them over the top.

8. Serve.

TIP: Freezing these is key! Do not skip that step!

PEANUT BUTTER COOKIE POPS

Makes 30

1 package Nutter Butter cookies

One 8-ounce block cream cheese, softened

1 pound white almond bark

30 paper straws

We are not fancy eaters in my house, but I am a bit of a food snob when it comes to one food—cookies. See, I prefer warm cookies right out of the oven, or those soft frosted cookies you get at the grocery store. Crunchy cookies you buy from the store? Not cool, bro. However, my grandma keeps Nutter Butters in her pantry, and those are one crunchy cookie I will go to town on, so it only made sense to smash 'em up, mix them with cream cheese, and make Cookie Pops. These are so amazing you might want to double the recipe!

1. Add all the cookies except two to a food processor and crush finely. Add the cream cheese to the cookies and blend until they are combined.

2. Roll the cookie mixture into 1-inch balls and place them on a wax paper-lined tray. Place a paper straw in each ball.

3. Place the tray in the freezer for 1 hour or more.

4. Microwave the almond bark in 30-second increments until it is fully melted.

5. Remove the cookie balls from the freezer and dip one by one into the almond bark, tapping off the excess. Place them back on the wax-lined tray.

6. Finely crush the two reserved cookies and sprinkle them over the top.

7. Serve.

TIP: I like to dip these in the white almond bark, but they are just as delicious in chocolate!

S'MORES RICE CRISPY CAKE

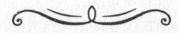

Serves 8 to 10

3 cups crisped rice cereal

3 cups graham cereal

10 ounces marshmallows

1 cup chocolate chips

3 tablespoons butter or margarine

Crushed graham cereal, hot fudge, and mini marshmallows, for decoration (optional)

TIP: Use a serrated knife to slice this cake up perfectly.

My mom and grandma love rice crispy treats. My grandma makes them with peanuts (oh my god, *yum*) and my mom makes them plain, but not often since she can't rest until the whole pan is gone. One day I got the crazy idea to take all that marshmallowy goodness and pack it into a Bundt pan, and out popped a rice crispy cake. Craziness, right?

I love the flavor of s'mores but I don't like the actual execution. Without fail, every time I take a bite the molten marshmallow busts out the other side and lands right on my toes. Then the rest of the marshmallow sticks to my face, and my hair decides it wants to join that party, and when I go to move my hair, it sticks to my fingers. It's not worth it. This cake gets to the s'mores flavor in a cleaner, less sticky way. Bits of graham cereal and chocolate chips mix with the marshmallows to pack the cake with all the campfirey goodness of s'mores.

1. Grease a Bundt pan.
2. Microwave the marshmallows and butter in a large microwave-safe bowl in 30-second increments until they are melted and smooth.
3. Immediately add the cereal and chocolate chips to the marshmallow mixture and mix to combine. Add the mixture to the Bundt pan and pack down into the pan evenly.
4. Let the mixture cool completely and stiffen up, about an hour in the fridge.
5. Transfer the cake from the pan onto a plate. You can stop here or decorate further.
6. To decorate, drizzle hot fudge down the sides and sprinkle with mini marshmallows and crushed graham cereal. Slice and serve.

BANANA SPLIT CHEESECAKE COOKIE BITES

Makes 2 dozen

One 17.5-ounce pouch sugar cookie mix

1 egg

8 tablespoons (1 stick) butter, softened

One 8-ounce block cream cheese, softened

1 tablespoon granulated sugar

One 5.1-ounce package banana instant pudding

1½ cups milk

Hot fudge

Sprinkles

24 maraschino cherries

TIP: To change it up, try chocolate sugar cookie mix. You can fill little cookie cups with any flavor of creamy cheesecake filling. I make them a million ways and each one is delicious.

My mom and husband both love bananas and they both love these Banana Split Cheesecake Cookie Bites. Creamy banana cheesecake filling is piped into sugar cookie cups before being drizzled with hot fudge and a cherry on top. Then I add sprinkles.

1. Preheat your oven to 350°F. Lightly grease a 24-well mini muffin tin.

2. In a bowl mix the sugar cookie mix with the egg and butter.

3. Roll the dough into about 1½-inch balls.

4. Place one dough ball in each muffin well. Spread the dough up the sides to form a cup.

5. Bake for 10 to 12 minutes, until the dough is lightly browned.

6. Remove the tin from the oven and, while it is still warm, use a spoon or little shot glass to press down the middle of each cookie cup, re-forming the cup shape. Let them cool.

7. Beat together the cream cheese and the sugar in a large bowl using a hand mixer.

8. In a separate bowl, mix the pudding mix and the milk.

9. Add the pudding mixture to the cream cheese mixture and stir to combine.

10. Spoon the cheesecake filling into a zip-top or piping bag. If using a zip-top bag, cut off one corner of the bag to make a makeshift piping bag.

11. Remove the cooled cups from the pan and fill them with filling.

12. Drizzle the cups with hot fudge, add sprinkles, and top with a cherry!

13. Refrigerate for 30 minutes before serving.

You should always add sprinkles because sprinkles make people happy—you try being sad around those colorful little bits of sugar. They are a fabulous way to add color and make any dessert look amazing. Not only are sprinkles delicious and colorful (and just awesome), but they also are a good way to jazz up bland-looking desserts, to cover up mistakes, or to draw attention away from the fact your cake came out a little crooked. Sprinkles fix everything!

PIG PICKIN' TRES LECHES CAKE

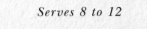

Serves 8 to 12

One 15-ounce box yellow cake mix

1 cup water (or amount indicated on cake mix directions)

3 eggs (or amount indicated on cake mix directions)

⅓ cup oil (or amount indicated on cake mix directions)

⅓ cup milk

One 12-ounce can evaporated milk

One 14-ounce can sweetened condensed milk

One 8-ounce container Cool Whip

One 8-ounce can crushed pineapple, drained

One 11-ounce can mandarin oranges, drained

8 to 10 maraschino cherries

TIP: You can also decorate the top with maraschino cherries, just to make it "purty!"

Every summer when I was younger my grandparents would have a pig pickin'. For anyone who doesn't know what a pig pickin' is, it's exactly what it sounds like! A whole pig spends the entire day roasting outside, driving all the swimmers crazy with its delicious aroma. And while there was the pork and tables full of homemade potato salad, deviled eggs, and mac and cheese, the star of the meal for me was the pig pickin' cake. This classic cake is one of my all-time favorites. Yellow cake mix is prepared with the addition of mandarin oranges. The cake is frosted with the most heavenly combination of Cool Whip, crushed pineapple, and mandarin oranges. It is kept in the fridge so it's always cool, creamy, and just amazing!

The cool creaminess of my family's pig pickin' cake reminded me of another of my favorite cakes—tres leches—and it seemed like common sense to put the two together to make one utterly amazing, super simple dessert. And you don't have to roast a whole pig to enjoy this cake—it's great for any get-together or BBQ!

1. Preheat your oven to 350°F. Lightly grease a 9-by-13-inch baking dish.

2. Make and bake the cake in the greased baking dish according to the box directions.

3. Let the cake cool slightly and poke holes all over the cake with a fork.

4. Mix together the milk, evaporated milk, and sweetened condensed milk until they are combined. Pour the milk mixture all over the cake.

5. Mix the Cool Whip with the crushed pineapple. Ice the top of the cake with the Cool Whip mixture.

6. Decorate the top of the cake with the mandarin oranges and cherries.

7. Refrigerate for 4 hours before serving.

❧ ACKNOWLEDGMENTS ❧

I want to take a few minutes to thank everyone that made this book possible.

A big thank you to my husband, for wrangling the kids for me so I could work; for getting me all the takeout tacos I could eat on the nights I was too exhausted to cook; for cleaning up the kitchen after it looked like a tornado had hit; for supporting me and pushing me even when I wanted to give up; and for believing in me and being my biggest fan. I love you, babe.

To my mom, who has worked so hard to support me and my brother and sister so we can accomplish these dreams of ours. And for coming home after working all day to help with the boys while I cooked.

To my sister, for spending her days watching Sam while I furiously typed and cooked. And for being the hand in most of my photos.

To my boys, Sam and Dean: they are the loves of my life, my babies, my boys. They inspire me and motivate me to work harder so I can give them the world they deserve.

To my grandma, who introduced me to cooking, Martha Stewart, and our family recipes. She deserves a big thank you for spending a week at my house, morning to night, helping me bake and cook up all the recipes for the photos in this book. She cleaned my kitchen continuously while I worked and ran out to get any food I forgot. Without her I would still be shooting.

I have a huge family and to thank them all would fill this book. They are my biggest supporters and my favorite taste testers.

Thank you to all of my blogger friends for their support and for being such great inspirations.

Of course I have to thank my readers at *Life with the Crust Cut Off* for helping me grow and be able to do what I love, and for making it possible for me to make this cookbook dream of mine come true!

Lastly, thank you to Ann Treistman and Aurora Bell at Countryman Press for making this dream a reality.

I love you all!

❧ INDEX ❧